You Are Destined for Greatness

HAMMER DOWN !

Aaron Putze

YOU

ARE DESTINED FOR

STORIES OF INSPIRATION & EMPOWERMENT

GREATNESS

bpc

ISBN-13: 978-1-950790-99-9
Business Publications Corporation Inc., Des Moines, IA

Business Publications Corporation Inc.
The Depot at Fourth
100 4th Street
Des Moines, Iowa 50309
(515) 288-3336

YOU ARE DESTINED FOR GREATNESS

"I've always tried to be the best. I've never been known as a quitter. I think that's contributed more to my success than anything else."

HAP PETERSON, IOWA HAWKEYE, IN A CONVERSATION WITH MIKE HLAS, CEDAR RAPIDS GAZETTE, OCT. 16, 1985

Dedicated to my wife Crystal and children Garrett, Grant and Jaelyn for your tremendous support and encouragement!

And to my mother Rita for inspiring, teaching and overcoming. You are the ultimate role model!

INTRODUCTION
You Are Destined for Greatness

YOU are destined for greatness.

Yes, *you*.

And your best friend, spouse, neighbor, and co-worker.

And the person standing next to you preparing to board the 6 a.m. red-eye from Des Moines to Chicago.

Greatness is there for us to grab hold of. What's exciting is that it comes in all forms and callings: from being an awesome parent, helpful classmate, valued colleague, or nationally recognized athlete to holding elected office, earning a diploma, leading a not-for-profit, or starting a business.

The opportunity for fulfillment that comes with doing remarkable things is ever present, provided we want it bad enough to work for honestly. Best of all, we can lead from where we're at and at this very moment. That's empowering! That's awesome!

This book can help.

•

Collecting stories, experiences, and inspirational memes from more than two dozen notable and accomplished leaders was itself a journey!

It began in Spring 2015 when I asked Iowa Hawkeyes' great Chuck Long if someone had captured his remarkable career in a book. He had just been named executive director of the Iowa Sports Foundation and was someone I had always admired as a fan of college football. I mean, why not? His story is an amazing one. The kid who averaged just a few tosses a game as QB for a high school team that featured the run and wound up setting every passing record for the University of Iowa,

Chuck Long, QB, Iowa Hawkeyes *(University of Iowa Athletic Communications)*

finishing runner-up in the 1985 Heisman Trophy race and being selected in the first round of the '86 NFL Draft. How cool is that?

Much to my surprise, his response was "no." Seriously? The legend was without a book and since no one was getting any younger or memories any sharper, it was important to get one started and published.

Chuck agreed. Nearly 1,000 hours of research, writing and editing later (a journey that included sifting through several thousand newspaper clippings his parents Charlie and Joan had stashed away in the basement of the family's home in Wheaton, Illinois), *Destined for Greatness* was published Nov. 6, 2017.

Developing the Chuck Long narrative included conversations with Iowa football coaches Hayden Fry and Kirk Ferentz, Chuck's wife Lisa, mother Joan and brother David, Iowa Governor (and now U.S. Ambassador to China) Terry Branstad and Chuck Long's teammates Hap Peterson and Mark Vlasic. As the manuscript evolved, an additional chapter appeared capturing many of the leadership principles that surfaced during the conversations.

Intrigued with the insights obtained, I ventured off the beaten path, visiting with leaders and mentors in finance, retail, academia, media, and business. With each request I made for interviews, more doors opened, and the chapter grew. Then it grew some more. Before long, it warranted its own book. *You Are Destined for Greatness* was the result.

•

It was quite a journey that led from one book to another. Life is a journey, too. It features twists and turns, and is affected by many internal and external forces.

Internally, we're talking about the human spirit. It's powerful, and burns continuously. Think of it like a pilot light: allow it to grow dim, and it will. Conversely, the human spirit burns brightly if we regularly fuel it with positive energy from external sources, which include our varied experiences and interactions with others.

Think of it this way: We're surrounded by a vast horizon of opportunity that stretches as far as our eye can see and our minds can comprehend. It's unprecedented, really, and within that space are endless ways to communicate, connect, learn, discover, and explore. We can try all kinds of things, partake of all kinds of experiences, and meet all kinds of people – the possibilities are truly staggering. They're even accessible from the comfort of your favorite recliner.

What connects the two—the human spirit within us and the boundless opportunity surrounding us—is *choice*. For better or worse, the choices we make either nourish or dim the spirit that burns within us. The choices we make also have a profound impact on others and the world around us.

So many choices, indeed. Will I work hard? Put in the effort? Get up early? Study late? Respect others? Rise to the occasion? Listen to understand? Stand for something? Volunteer? Do the right thing? Try again when I fail? Hang with people who are going places?

Or will I choose to cut corners? Settle? Coast? Be reckless? Make excuses? Give in? Give up?

With countless "reality" shows saturating culture, it's easy to forget that the choices we make have real consequences. Make bad choices and bad stuff usually happens. Ask yourself, "Do the choices I make enable me to capitalize on the opportunities that come my way?" Or, do poor choices stymie true success and happiness?

You're destined for greatness. Seizing that greatness is up to you. Make good choices and you put yourself in a position to make the most of the opportunity when it presents itself. The funny thing is, opportunity often arrives without warning or fanfare.. If we're not prepared, we might not recognize it when it comes. But whatever you do, don't cave. Don't be paralyzed by self-doubt. Don't set arbitrary limits on your potential or be tempted into thinking there are shortcuts. Don't believe you are undeserving of fulfillment and the good things that accompany success.

Instead, go out. Create. Be different. Make the people around you want to be better. You have the power to do amazing things *and* be happy. The personal accounts of those featured within these pages are proof.

Just ask Chuck Long. He never expected to take the field as a starting quarterback in the National Football League. The boy from Wheaton North (Illinois) High School threw just 92 passes his senior season on a team, and for a coach, that featured the run. Recruited by only three universities, he went with his gut and signed with a relatively new coach at the University of Iowa named Hayden Fry. Five years later, he placed second to Auburn University's Bo Jackson for the Heisman Trophy, held eight passing records for the Hawkeyes, and was a first-round NFL draft pick for the Detroit Lions. He went on to coach college football, establish a foundation to aide those with cerebral palsy, and is currently motivating more than 250,000 Iowans to live longer and healthier lives as executive director of the Iowa Sports Foundation.

Or strike up a conversation with Bob Myers, and you'll quickly understand the power of commitment and perseverance. At age 41, and after serving 22 years in the U.S. Army, Bob returned home to Des Moines, Iowa and accepted an offer from his old high school friend, Don Lamberti, to go to work for Casey's General Store. He didn't even ask the starting salary. Instead, he threw himself into the job directing construction of the company's new corporate headquarters in Ankeny, Iowa. Over the next 25 years, Myers served as Chief Executive Officer. His leadership helped the Iowa-based food and fuel retailer grow from

Bob Myers

500 stores and 5,000 employees to nearly 2,000 stores and more than 33,000 employees with a presence in 14 states—and growing!

Visit a minute or two with John Quinn, who played quarterback for the Iowa State University Cyclones (1977-81) while earning a degree in accounting. He didn't want to fail in anything he attempted, but the son of an FBI agent nevertheless pivoted from business to pursuing a career in law enforcement. He took on the role of director of the Iowa Division of Criminal Investigation only to be demoted several years later. Undeterred, he applied for the Chief of Police for the City of Waukee, Iowa, but was turned down for the job before even being interviewed. Still persisting, he was offered the position one month later. Today, he helps protect the life, safety, and property of the nearly 20,000 residents living in one of the nation's fastest-growing cities. His goal for the department is no less ambitious: "To be the most successful law enforcement department in the state."

What do Chuck, Bob, John, not to mention Iowa State University President Wendy Wintersteen, U.S. Ambassador to China (and Iowa's

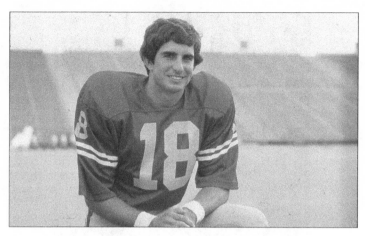

John Quinn, QB, Iowa State University Cyclones (1977-81)

longest-serving governor) Terry Branstad, Randy Edeker of Hy-Vee, Anderson-Erickson Dairy's CEO (and Chief Taste Tester!) Miriam Erickson Brown, Iowa Lottery CEO Terry Rich, and all exceptional leaders have in common? For starters, integrity. Also, an inner spirit that exudes conviction and strength. A service-oriented attitude. Continuous preparation and supreme self-confidence and work ethic. A love of what they do and an eagerness to take on new challenges. They're OK with failure. They don't shrink on the big stage but relish the platform it provides to do great things.

•

We're all destined for greatness. But the opportunity for greatness doesn't self-announce with billboards, flashing lights, or Burma Shave signs. As Jim Knuth, Sr. Vice President of Farm Credit Services of America, who played football at Iowa State University, says: "It is choice, not chance, that determines our destiny."

What are you doing *right now* to shape your future? What are you doing day in and day out to create opportunity, be seen as valuable, earn a promotion, or receive a job offer—maybe for a job that doesn't yet exist? What are you doing *today* to be a mentor and respected by your peers or to transform an idea into a new product or service? What are you invested in *right now* that will enable you to start or grow a business, get elected, lead a police force, or run a multi-billion-dollar company? How are you molding yourself *right now* to be indispensable to someone and missed when you're not around?

Don't wait for success. Get ready *right now* to take the snap and be open to new challenges and new opportunities. Be confident in your abilities and work hard. Leave excuses on the sidelines and take an interest in someone else's successes. Care more about your team than yourself. Be unconventional. Outwork the competition.

In my conversations with those featured in this book, sixteen key leadership themes emerged (ironically, the number Chuck wore as an Iowa Hawkeye and Detroit Lion). The stories that bring each of them to life are powerful, practical and relevant for you and your success.

Dive in and be transformed.

FOREWORD
You Are Destined for Greatness

By Miriam Erickson Brown
CEO (and Chief taste tester!)
Anderson Erickson Dairy
Des Moines, Iowa

There is nothing more personal than leadership.

Maybe that's because as leaders, bits of ourselves and our personalities have rubbed off in our businesses and organizations.

As the leader of our third generation family owned dairy, I consider my role a reflection of who I truly am. In fact, Dark Chocolate Milk and Strawberry Rhubarb Pie Yogurt are both examples of my creativity...in dairy form.

All of us can be leaders in many ways. Throughout the pages of this book, we find stories of great leaders who have a balanced and disciplined approach to constantly improving in their role. If we are focused on humility and excellence, as many of these wonderful leaders are, we can have a truly tremendous impact.

The downside in all of this is that our imperfections effect those we are leading. I should point out here that some of God's best work in my own life has been through my inadequacies and losses. After all, good leaders possess an authenticity that is irresistible and relatable. Maybe that's because the realness of their life stories shines through.

A leader is also a steward. They are a protector and defender of excellence and truth in their organization. Stewardship is a powerful force and something that doesn't get its due recognition.

In an organization, it really is the art of staying true to the greater purpose. It requires constant re-balancing and the wisdom to determine what the right thing to do is...and is not. It is lonely. Often, the leader is the only one who has the information and vision to determine the best course of action. Because so few understand this about leadership, it's an open invitation to be challenged.

Leaders must be masters of their trade yet remain open minded.

We must be unflappable but full of passion.

We need to remain flexible but uncompromising in our standards of excellence.

We are communicators of vision yet realists in choosing wisely what we share and when.

We face a tornado of information, but we must make sure to carefully select the right combination of things to make our businesses and organizations successful and engaging.

There is no one best recipe for successful leadership, but great leaders exist nonetheless. My prayer for you is that you nurture, honor, grow and protect your leadership role just as those in the stories on the pages that follow have done.

Inspiration is contagious.

Warmly,

Miriam Erickson Brown

Miriam Erickson Brown

"Never be afraid to raise your hand."

TERRY RICH, IOWA LOTTERY PRESIDENT AND CEO (RETIRED),
INTERNATIONAL SPEAKER, AUTHOR, SERIAL ENTREPRENEUR
AND ALL AROUND GOOD GUY, ON THE SECRET TO GETTING
THINGS DONE AND MAKING A DIFFERENCE

YOU ARE DESTINED FOR GREATNESS
FEATURING (IN ALPHABETICAL ORDER)

Terry Branstad, U.S. Ambassador to China

Miriam Erickson Brown, Anderson Erickson Dairy CEO

John Campbell, KCRG-TV Sports Director (retired)

Gary Dolphin, Voice of the Iowa Hawkeyes

Randy Edeker, Hy-Vee Inc. Chairman, CEO and President

Kirk Ferentz, Iowa Hawkeyes' Head Football Coach

Dr. Angela L. Walker Franklin, PhD, Des Moines University President

Hayden Fry, Iowa Hawkeyes' Head Football Coach (retired)

Bruce Harreld, University of Iowa President

Jonathan Hayes, Former collegiate and National Football League player and coach

Jim Knuth, Farm Credit Services of America Sr. Vice President

Chuck Long, Iowa Sports Foundation Executive Director and Big Ten Network Analyst

David Long, Zia Trust, Inc. VP and Sr. Trust Officer

Gene Meyer, Greater Des Moines Partnership President

Bob Myers, Casey's General Stores Inc. Chief Executive Officer (retired)

Angie Peterson, Children's Therapy Center of the Quad Cities President and CEO

Hap Peterson, The Hortus Group - AFORCE Recruiting Managing Partner

John Quinn, Waukee (Iowa) Chief of Police

Suku Radia, Bankers Trust Company Chief Executive Officer (retired)

Scott Raecker, The Robert D. and Billie Ray Center Executive Director

Bruce Rastetter, Entrepreneur

Doug Reichardt, Iowa Sports Foundation Chairman of the Board

Terry Rich, Iowa Lottery President and CEO (retired), speaker and author

John Streif, Iowa Hawkeyes Assistant Athletic Trainer (retired)

Kirk Tyler, Atlantic Coca-Cola Bottling Company President

Mark Vlasic, Mariner Wealth Advisors Sr. Wealth Advisor and former NFL QB

Wendy Wintersteen, Iowa State University President

1 Strength in Humility

"I just believe he's one of those people destined for greatness."

That prediction was made by Iowa head football coach Hayden Fry about Chuck Long before the Wheaton native even took a game-day snap as a Hawkeye. Destined for greatness?

Chuck Long, the lanky, curly blond-haired, sophomore-to-be quarterback yet to start a college football game? Really? Many were understandably surprised at the proclamation. First among them, Chuck.

"I think he's over exaggerating," Chuck replied when asked by sports writers to comment on Hayden's lofty prediction. "I haven't stepped on the field yet. I have a lot to prove. The entire offense has a lot to prove."

Chuck's humility became one of his most recognized assets as a football player and person. Perhaps that's because it's in such short supply.

In today's loud, noisy world, being humble is often considered risky. Questions abound. "Will I be noticed?" "Will I be rewarded?" "Will I be recognized?" "Will I be popular?"

The self-doubt is understandable, especially when pop culture encourages and celebrates a "me-first" attitude.

Leaders don't fall for it. In the real world, humility is strength. Keeping your feet firmly planted on the ground and having confidence in who you are are admirable qualities that lead to good things. The key is to be patient. Good things will happen to those who put others' needs first.

Randy Edeker, Chairman, CEO and President of Hy-Vee Inc. based in West Des Moines knows this first-hand. He is a continual study of role models. Some, he admits, are good. Others, not so much.

"Like a defensive player on a football team that's down 27 points who, when finally making a good hit on an opposing player who's already scored three touchdowns, dances around on the field before posing for the cameras," says Edeker. "As he does, I'm thinking, 'Hey buddy, you're down 27 points; there's nothing to be pounding your chest about.' But I think that's mainstream today. That's seen as success. Be as big and boastful as you possibly can."

Edeker is wise in his assessment. And who can argue with the success achieved by Edeker and Hy-Vee, the latter a true Iowa success story that arose from very humble beginnings.

Randy Edeker, Hy-Vee Chairman, CEO and President (left) talking food with U.S. Ag Secretary, former Iowa governor and Mt. Pleasant native Tom Vilsack (2013).

"Too often, young people believe they won't be successful if they are humble," he says. "I think the quiet kid sits and thinks, 'There's no way I'll succeed unless I make a lot of noise and talk the most and have the grandest plan.' But I just don't see that. For some young people, it takes time to get your footing. I think that's part of the issue. Young people need to see that it's OK to be humble. And those who are should be rewarded."

You'd think it would be easy for the leader of a super-successful grocery and fuel retailer to let success go to his head. But not Edeker. He relishes the importance of humility and encourages youth to embrace it.

"Being humble gets you a long way," he advises. "I once had the opportunity to sit with one of our great leaders, Richard Mitchell. He was this iconic, right-hand-man to Ron Pearson, Hy-Vee Chairman and CEO, serving as Sr. Vice President and Chief Administrative Officer. He was kind of the guy who told Ron what he needed to hear and when he needed to hear it."

Edeker tells the story: "Richard was retiring and I asked if he had any advice for me. He said, 'Randy, always go through the door last. Always sit in the back seat even when they want you to sit in the front. Always say 'please,' always say 'thank you' and always smile.'

"Now, those aren't hard things; those aren't big things. But he said that's the way you conduct yourself. If you start with that—because there are another 20 things you need to do to be successful—but if you start there, people will respect you. They'll listen to you and feel comfortable around you. Humility is the place to start. If you begin there, the rest will come easier and you'll avoid many pitfalls."

Edeker recalls attending a *Des Moines Register's* All-Iowa High School Sports Awards banquet and observing former Iowa football and National Football League quarterback Chuck Long.

"I'm seated with Peyton Manning and we're enjoying conversation and the atmosphere and having a good time. Obviously, he's a great role model as is Chuck.

"Throughout the evening, I'm watching Peyton and taking it all in. As the event concludes, Chuck sees me, comes over and introduces himself for like the 15th time – I mean, I'm literally thinking, 'I know who Chuck Long is. I was there. At the football games, when Chuck was on the field, leading Iowa to win after win; so for me, Chuck Long is a big deal. And yet, he comes up and says, 'Randy, Chuck Long.'

"And after we visited, I asked myself what that must be like for Chuck, to be at an event when you have another high-profile quarterback the likes of Peyton Manning, who, fresh off a Super Bowl victory with the Denver Broncos, is at the head table and getting all the limelight? Now, Chuck's not at the head table. And what must that be like?

"It's a lesson about humility, that's what it is," Edeker says. "It's doing the right thing. I watched him that night. What I noticed is that it wasn't about him wanting to come up and say 'Hey, hey, hey – notice me.' And he didn't first go up to Peyton and say, 'Hey Peyton, I'm Chuck Long.' Instead, he talked to the people he knew and the people he's around.

Edeker admits that he's not easily enamored with celebrities. He'd rather talk to the people he knows and is going to live and work with.

"But I watched Chuck that evening and again admired that characteristic of humility. He's a great person, a humble person and he remembers where he came from. Those who aspire to be leaders can learn a lot from how these men carry themselves."

Suku Radia isn't afraid to have fun, evident by his retirement party held in 2017. "True leaders are inquisitive," Radia says. "They never stop asking questions and continuously seek advice and input. They ask for information and listen. They consider issues from all sides." From left: Don Coffin, CEO Bankers Trust; Barry Griswell, retired CEO, Principal Financial Group; Suku; Ken Arlen and Mike Avery of the Ken Arlen Orchestra.

Retired Bankers Trust Company Chief Executive Officer Suku Radia says true leadership starts with humility. Without it, companies and individuals are doomed to fail.

"If you don't have humility, leadership will be short-lived," says the community servant who led Bankers Trust for nine years before retiring in December 2017. "Think about it. When you really get right down to it, if you have a big ego and you become a leader, your big ego will destroy the organization's culture."

As CEO of Bankers Trust, Radia always sat with his team at the same table when they met. He didn't stand at the head of the table and dictate orders. He didn't even tell his team his own idea on most of the matters they discussed.

"I wasn't going to express an opinion for one simple reason: if I did, they would say, 'Oh yeah, this is what Suku wants and he's our CEO so let's rally behind it.' But you know what? I didn't have the market cornered on good decisions. I wanted to have discussion. I wanted to hear other voices. *If you're humble, step back and let other talented people take the lead, they will come to the right decision*."

•

"Our parents (Charlie and Joan) modeled humility. Dad never said a word about his success as a high school basketball player. And mom never told us about her academic success. Yet I eventually came to learn by other family members that she was a tremendous student. She made straight-As all the way through school, and that included two years in the Ivy League at Wellesley. We knew she was very smart and made excellent grades throughout school, but you literally had to pull it from her or from other family members. Humility was a big part of what was modeled and how we grew up."

DAVID LONG, BROTHER OF CHUCK LONG

•

It's hard to be humble. And that's particularly true for those who have supreme self-confidence. Knowing how to navigate the fine line between confidence and arrogance takes work, but that skill can be mastered.

"I used to struggle with that," admits Des Moines University President Dr. Angela Walker Franklin. "I don't think anyone has ever described me as 'arrogant,' but perhaps looking back in my earlier years, I could have been seen as controlling because I was very organized and very deliberate in what I did in my approach to doing things."

Franklin recalls being the person others would ask to convene a meeting and prepare an agenda.

Dr. Angela Walker Franklin (center) believes in collaboration and civility. As Des Moines University president, she founded a discussion series titled "Opposing Views: Finding Common Ground." It provides students an open forum for discussing issues freely and civilly. "Arguing is an ineffective approach to problem solving," says Franklin.

"People would say I was controlling but that reputation got me into a lot of leadership roles. It went from controlling to being 'the VOR'—or the 'voice of reason'—because I soon became the person who could get things done."

But the more Franklin evolved in her career, the more she learned about the need to bring others along with her.

"People respected that I wanted everyone to be part of it and to be part of success. Leaders bring others with them. It can never be just about you. It's about bringing everyone along and embracing everyone and ensuring that they are part of the plan and the results and the success."

Today, Franklin continues to adjust her approach. She has evolved from telling her employees how something is going to get done to asking them how they think it should be done.

"This is a subtle change of approach but it matters," Franklin says. "Being a leader is about asking the right questions of others. I like the approach of being deliberate and talking through what can be done together. I'm not here to be served; I will roll up my sleeves and get in there like everyone else and we work it out together. So this idea of being controlling shifted to being engaging. Leaders need to be seen as engaging and actively involved. Then, surround yourself with people who are key leaders who are accountable but have the ability to make decisions and be major players on the team."

Kirk Tyler, CEO and Chairman of the Atlantic Bottling Company, says the wrong kind of leadership is the person who says, "I'm the boss and I know more than everyone else." In reality: the best ideas come from within a team.

Tyler knows from experience. Raised in Atlantic, Iowa, his father Jim helped operate two bottling plants, one in their hometown and the other in Creston. By the time he was a senior in high school, Tyler had done nearly every job in the plant – from sweeping floors to sorting bottles.

"All the jobs that others didn't want to do," he says with a wry smile.

That experience has helped Tyler relate to every member of the team – and to welcome their input.

"Not being humble and open to what other people have to share is one of the biggest mistakes you can make if you aspire to be a leader," Tyler warns. "***You'll miss out on a lot of good ideas when you think you're the only one who has them.***"

Humility is at the core of being successful in business and life, says retired Casey's General Stores Inc. Chief Executive Officer Bob Myers.

"I'm delighted that in this country and particularly in the business world in this modern day, the focus has turned to the importance of leadership development," he says. "Leadership includes many things, but at its heart is being humble in all we do."

"Few could have imagined the growth of Atlantic Bottling Co. but we've worked hard and tried to keep things simple," says Kirk Tyler pictured left with his father Jim and son Jay (1996). Today, it remains a privately owned, independent bottler and distributor of Coca-Cola products doing business in Iowa, Illinois, Wisconsin, Minnesota and Missouri. The company operates from nine Iowa locations with its headquarters still located in Atlantic, Iowa.

Humility is about putting others first. Myers, a Des Moines native and military veteran who retired from his role with Casey's in December 2016, offers advice every servant leader should heed.

"One thing I really wanted to do during my time at Casey's was to know every employee by their first name and a little about their families—all 33,000," he says. "If you wanted to see a power unleashed, that would be it right there.

"Obviously, I wasn't able to do that as much as I would have liked, but I tried, aware of how it would empower and set an example for others."

Bob Myers, Casey's General Stores Inc. Chief Executive Officer (retired)

•

"For me personally, faith is a motivator and a driver that helps keep me humble. From a leadership standpoint, being driven and passionate and having a positive impact on the lives of others starts with loving your neighbor like yourself. The neighbor may be the person next door or across the ocean who doesn't have a safe way to deliver a baby or a roof over their head or a school to attend. Always ask, 'Is the life I'm living one that positively impacts others?' I don't know how best to describe it because some of the most overused clichés are faith, family and friends. But it's always good to take inventory of your priorities."

SCOTT RAECKER, EXECUTIVE DIRECTOR,
THE ROBERT D. AND BILLIE RAY CENTER, DRAKE UNIVERSITY

•

Leaders aren't born, says Bruce Harreld, University of Iowa president.

"Leadership is experiential. The more experience and the more failures you have, the more you learn and the better you're going to be."

But guard against going it alone and hoarding the spotlight for yourself.

"You can get to the point where you become arrogant," says Harreld. "You need to catch yourself and say, 'Hey, wait a minute, do I need help here? Is there someone else here who knows more than I do?' The answer is almost always yes."

•

John Quinn, Waukee, Iowa's, chief of police, echos the importance of faith and the humility that comes from being a faith-filled person.

"Faith is critical. It's the core of humility. It's knowing there's something greater than you who has a plan for you and will support you and provide the tools you need to be a success. I've been blessed. I've done things that people have dreamed about and written books about. But I've remained grounded because of my faith and my family."

•

"My experience is that a lot of stuff starts at home. All of us are products of our environment. But I think people innately and generally want to do well. They want to learn and want to be coached. As a coach, teacher and parent, you must invest time in them and show them that you're genuinely trying to help them be better. You want to always look for humble players because humble guys want to be coached."

KIRK FERENTZ, HEAD FOOTBALL COACH, IOWA HAWKEYES

•

In this day of 'me first,' humility must be coached to athletes at all levels.

Hap Peterson, a first team, all-state defensive lineman for Bettendorf who was recruited to Iowa in 1981 by Coach Hayden Fry, doesn't always like what he observes.

Hap Peterson (right) with his college football coach Hayden Fry of the Iowa Hawkeyes, spring 2018 at Hayden's residence in suburban Dallas-Fort Worth (photo by Joseph L. Murphy).

"Unfortunately, too many parents are raising kids to fulfill dreams they can't," says Peterson, a Bettendorf native and Iowa City resident. "That's not lost on a lot of people. I get it, I've seen it. And it just ruins people."

Peterson is a firm believer that kids have to live their lives and do their things.

"I've never put pressure on my kids to be in athletics or excel in sports. My expectation is for them to do their own thing and find their own way. I had my time and I had my passion and I did things my way. They got to do it their way now."

Too often, however, Hap sees the fun of sports literally being taken away from kids because of the pressure placed on them by parents. This especially holds true as they move up the ranks and prepare for college.

"I get it. The cost of an education is so high these days that sports can be a means to an end," he admits. "But my advice is that whatever you do and your kids do, be sure to do it for all the right reasons and be humble as you do it.

"If you have a motivation and passion, than playing sports to earn that scholarship can be the means to an end in terms of getting an education. And that's great. But if not, then turn your time and talents elsewhere."

•

"I share with young people that we should strive to first be kind in whatever role we play. Being kind is incredibly important. Leadership is about love and being kind. We would be so much more effective and successful as individuals and a country if we first strived to be kind to one another."

WENDY WINTERSTEEN, IOWA STATE UNIVERSITY PRESIDENT

•

Gene Meyer is synonymous with all things greater Des Moines and Central Iowa.

He serves as president of the Greater Des Moines Partnership, has been mayor of West Des Moines, and is often asked to serve on boards and committees. But it's family that means the most to him. It also keeps him grounded.

Gene (right) with his family at daughter, Abby's, wedding (from left: Adam, Matthew, Abby, Kathy)

"You'll see an award when you walk into my office," he says, motioning toward his home away from home. "It looks like an Emmy Award of me being a 'Father of the Year.'

"It was one or two years ago when I sat at a banquet and watched a video in which my children talked about me. And I have never been so humbled in my life. The things they said about me or the things they said I did for them aren't things that I could write down on a piece of paper. What I just tried to do was to be there for them, provide them direction, but with freedom."

•

From the Author

Humility. It's a rare commodity today. So when it shines, you notice.

Such was the case when I met Harrison Barnes July 11, 2014 at the Summer Iowa Games opening ceremonies held in his hometown of Ames, Iowa.

Aaron Putze (right) with NBA star and former Ames High prep standout Harrison Barnes at the Iowa Sport's Foundation's Summer Iowa Games Athlete Jamboree in Ames (July 2014).

The athlete had every reason to be walking on air—and to have his nose in it, too. Barnes had helped lead Ames High School to back-to-back undefeated seasons and Class 4-A State Basketball Championships his junior and senior seasons as a Little (Ames) Cyclone. He had his pick of offers from elite men's college basketball programs, ultimately choosing to take the hardwood as a North Carolina Tar Heel.

In two seasons under the tutelage of coach Roy Williams, Barnes averaged more than 16 points per game, scored 40 points vs. Clemson in an ACC Tournament game as a freshman (most ever by a first-year player), earned ACC Rookie of the Year recognition, and helped lead North Carolina to two consecutive NCAA Men's Basketball Elite 8 appearances.

In 2012, he was selected by the Golden State Warriors as the 7th pick in the National Basketball Association's (NBA) draft. His professional resume included scoring 26 points as a rookie in a second-round NBA playoff game and being selected to the 2012-13 All-Rookie NBA first team. In 2015, he helped win an NBA Championship for Golden State by playing in tandem with dynamic guard Steph Curry and sharpshooter Klay Thompson.

Despite that kind of resume, you'd be hard-pressed to find a more humble and sincere person than Harrison.

At no time did that humility shine brighter than during his keynote speech to the athletes of all ages who filled the west stands of Jack Trice Stadium on the Iowa State University Campus on a warm, July summer evening.

I listened intently as Harrison spoke with purpose and passion. His words resonated with me as a father and as someone raised on a farm near West Bend, Iowa, who attended a small school and learned the lesson of hard work from my parents Edward and Rita—a quality that I was now diligently trying to pass along to my three children.

After completing his 10-minute keynote, Harrison accepted a warm round of applause and returned to a small bleacher where I was seated. As the applause subsided, I leaned in to Harrison and shared my words of admiration and appreciation for the message he gave and the spirit in which he gave it.

"And if I could kindly request," I added, "could I have a copy of the remarks you just delivered? I have three children who need to hear what you had to say."

Without hesitation, Harrison retrieved from his pocket a two-page, type written document and placed it in my hand.

"Of course," he replied. "And be sure to give them my best."

It read:

Thank you for that warm reception. I am so happy to be back here in Ames at the Iowa Games! Let me begin by telling you this. I admire you. Each and every one of you.

And it isn't because of the quality of your skills, or the athletic prowess that you possess. I am proud of you because you are here.

Today, and this week, you are making a statement to your family, to your friends and most importantly, to yourself, that you have drive. You have ambition. You have a strong work ethic. And that you know how to be part of a team.

I was sitting where you are, just a few years ago. My mother inspired me to play basketball at a young age and, when I was in fourth, fifth and sixth grade, I was fortunate enough to play in the Iowa Games. When I arrived here, I felt what you are feeling right now, that I made it to the big leagues. That I was on the big stage. I am here to tell you that you are feeling those butterflies and this excitement, because this really is your opportunity to see what the big platform feels like.

I can tell you that I felt the same way going into the Iowa Games as I did going in the National Basketball Association. The venue might have changed, but that feeling of purpose, of excitement, of adventure, stayed the same.

You will be facing the best athletes in the region. Look around. The kids that you meet during these Games will be the same ones that you will be competing against in middle school, high school and maybe even in college and the pros. The reason this feels like something special is because it IS something special: a foundation that will unite you all through your careers and through your lives.

It is here at the Iowa Games that I felt that for the first time, I was playing with a purpose. While I have always loved basketball, the Iowa Games opened me up to a whole new experience: one where winning a game felt like a major and tangible achievement. It was the first time that this sport ever made me feel like king of the world.

Like everything that has meaning, the road to your athletic success will be paved with difficult times. Being from Iowa, your game will be doubted. You will hear things like, "Well, in Iowa, the competition isn't that stiff. Let's see how you do when you face real competition." Or you will hear that you are from the Midwest and the athletes aren't as tough here as they are in the big cities.

I heard all of those things over and over again when I was playing in national high school all-star events. I heard them in college and I heard them when I went to the NBA. And for a while, it stung. I was constantly hearing "What else can you do? What else makes you special?" It felt like not only did I have to prove myself, but I had to prove my upbringing. But now, I can't help but smile when I hear them.

You see, people that aren't from the Midwest misunderstand our kind nature. They see our manners, how we treat our neighbors and they equate that with being soft.

They're wrong. There is strength in kindness. Courage in taking the high road. Valor in teamwork. Being a great competitor does not mean being a great trash talker. To be a great competitor, you must always strive to be better than others. I am going to let you in on a secret: you learn more than competing here at the Iowa Games. You will learn how to succeed when others might have more natural skills than you. You will learn how to keep your focus when your adrenaline is pumping and everything is riding on a single moment. You will learn how to test yourself. You will learn how to achieve while staying humble.

And whether you pursue a career in athletics or not, the Iowa Games will be here for you, to challenge you and to allow you to challenge yourself. This is an amazing experience and I am so glad you all get to experience it with each other. Play well, take it all in and have fun.

– Harrison Barnes

FROM HUMBLE BEGINNINGS TO INDUSTRY LEADER: THAT'S THE STORY OF HY-VEE

Hy-Vee traces its roots to 1930 and the small town of Beaconsfield, Iowa. Two men, Charles Hyde (1883-1970) and David Vredenburg (1884-1949), opened the Beaconsfield Supply Store (now listed on the National Register of Historic Places). The goal: offer patrons "good merchandise, appreciative service and low prices."

They say timing is everything. Well, almost everything! Hyde and Vredenburg leased their first store just weeks prior to the stock market crash of October 1929. But with faith, dogged determination and a belief that times would get better, they persevered. By 1938, the two men began calling their operation Hyde & Vredenburg and just five years later, they and 14 others incorporated 15 Iowa and Missouri stores bearing the same name. In 1952, the name Hy-Vee was born.

From those humble beginnings, Hy-Vee has flourished. Today, the employee-owned chain includes hundreds of grocery stores and drugstores located throughout the Midwestern United States in Iowa, Illinois, Kansas, Minnesota, Missouri, Nebraska, South Dakota, and Wisconsin. Their generosity is unmatched in the industry – from supporting Variety The Children's Charity, Juvenile Diabetes Research Foundation, The American Red Cross and Honor Flights to backing local, community-based activities too numerous to mention.

This success didn't just happen.

While many companies get distracted by the fear of failure, Hy-Vee has embraced the opportunities afforded by success by continually offering new approaches, services and offerings.

There are numerous examples in the company's nearly 90-year history.

Since its founding, Hy-Vee stores have operated autonomously, choosing their own inventories and setting their own prices. Store managers (now referred to as store directors) were then, and still are today, encouraged to test new ideas.

According to the company's website, one of the first such entrepreneurial concepts – employee bonuses – was introduced in 1936 and endures to this day.

In the 1940s, stores began offering customers the use of newly invented shopping carts. In 1957, their first in-store bakery began operations – the start of many in-store departments. The 1960s brought the establishment of an employee trust fund, the first Drug Town, introduction of the slogan "A Helpful Smile in Every Aisle," courtesy counter, dine-in area, delicatessen and first express lane checkout. Then came video rentals, bank branches in stores, pizza and the first free-standing floral department – all in the 1980s. Also in 1984, Hy-Vee made national news when it became the second store in the nation to offer customers the use of a debit card to pay for purchases.

Hy-Vee has continued to be an innovator ever since. In 1990, it introduced film processing and in 1992, the first Chinese Express department. By 1997, Hy-Vee was selling fuel. Then came the 2000s and in-store dieticians, the opening of gas stations, national attention brought by NFL quarterback and University of Northern Iowa graduate Kurt Warner (who previously had worked as a night stocker for Hy-Vee in Cedar Falls).

Not satisfied with the status-quo, Hy-Vee has continually redesigned its store interiors, expanded into baby, pets, cosmetics and additional general merchandise departments, redesigned its in-store restaurants, sponsored a triathlon and golf tournaments and launched a magazine. In 2015, Hy-Vee fully implemented its online grocery shopping program. Today, Hy-Vee remains Iowa's largest private employer – a distinction it's held since 1991.

From humble beginnings to continuous innovator, catalyst for community renewal and committed to 100-percent customer satisfaction. That's the Hy-Vee brand.

What's yours?

REFLECTIONS

Who needs encouragement and what can you do to provide it?

_____

_____

_____

_____

_____

_____

Who recently achieved a goal, award or promotion and how can you congratulate them for their success?

_____

_____

_____

_____

_____

_____

2 Shoot Straight

Do you follow through on your word? Do you meet deadlines, deliver on a promise, or fulfill a pledge? Can others believe you? Are you honest about who you are and how you feel?

Bottom line: can you be trusted? Or are you all talk?

Shooting straight is a hallmark of someone who can be counted on. Leaders are people who mean what they say and say what they mean.

Being honest about yourself and with others is a stepping stone to great achievements. Every leader featured in this book frequently referenced honesty while sharing their story and experiences.

Bob Myers, who retired as CEO of Casey's General Store in 2016 after 27 years with the company, didn't mince words when it came to the importance of backing up what you say with action.

The goal-oriented man with a military background and unmatched work ethic never hesitated to speak his mind professionally and honestly. His leadership is what helped create one of America's most successful, employee-centric companies.

Just months prior to celebrating his retirement, Bob reflected on his accomplishments from his office at the company's corporate headquarters in Ankeny, Iowa (appropriately located on "Convenience Blvd.").

Not surprisingly, Bob stressed the importance of trust, beginning with being true to family.

"It all starts there," he said with conviction. "You can never undersell the importance of being a trusted parent and conveying the importance of having good values to your children.

"And indeed, you may not think you're getting through to them as a parent, but you are. Hopefully it's a positive message that's rooted in honesty and being a straight shooter.

At some point and time, Bob adds, "you hope that that young person—if they have a nurturing and firm parental structure—that the young person will be of his own mind and not follow peer groups who don't have their best interest at heart just for the sake of following."

He then took the conversation to an even higher plane.

"There are many core elements to leadership and making good decisions. They include honesty, integrity, fairness and professionalism. Add to that the spirituality of the human component—your faith is your core—and you have those attributes that you should continually encourage and pass along to your children."

And this leads to serving others.

"The sense of fairness is one my father imparted on me and I didn't even realize it at the time," added Bob, who was raised in a modest, blue-collar neighborhood near Des Moines' Firestone plant. "*You want to leave this world a little bit better than when you came into it, even if it is just one person you've touched in a positive way*. These are the things we as parents and leaders have a responsibility of passing along to our children and grandchildren."

Although his father passed when Bob was just 11, the positive influence he modeled left a lasting impression. Lessons learned included being honest and truthful in all that you do and treating others fairly.

"Don't judge others by their skin color, ethnicity, or background. Evaluate them for who they are and what they can do," he says. "This sense of fairness was a driving force behind my father and I know I picked it up from him.

"Also, be honest in all that you do. I can remember mowing grass when I was nine or ten years old; somehow, some way he was imparting on me the need to work hard, establish relationships with people, and to put in an honest day's work for a fair wage.

"The kinds of values he imparted on me were very profound and stay with me to this very day."

•

Being a leader means being consistent—a straight shooter, says Gary Dolphin, voice of the Iowa Hawkeyes' football and men's basketball teams. After signing on with Iowa in December 1996, there was a 10-month build-up until the next Hawkeyes' sports season— from the press conference in December until football kicked off the following September.

Gary Dolphin (second from left) joining Chuck Hartlieb, Lon Olejniczak, Chuck Long, Jason Olejniczak and Aaron Putze at the La Poste in Perry, Iowa Dec. 19, 2018 for an event benefiting the Perry High School Blue Jays football team.

"This was far from ideal," Gary says, "as I would have preferred the season started the next week. You had all this build up and affiliate kissing and handshakes. I mean, I'm good with it, I get it. But I just wanted to move on and get into the booth."

To plan the transition from the old guard to new guard, several meetings were held with long-time and beloved Hawkeyes' sports announcer Jim Zabel and color men Bob Brooks and Ron Gonder. There was a professional tension in the room, at which time Gary took control.

"I remember saying, 'Look, guys, I'm not here to replace anybody. You know how this industry works. I'm here to do my job like you're here to do yours,'" he recalls. "My job, just like yours, will last a few years and then, all too soon, someone's going to come in and replace me. We're going to move on. You'll get your air time and your due. But just understand that once the game starts, it's my show. And I need to have your cooperation.'"

It was important to be honest and to shoot straight.

"It greatly helped my situation because we were testing new waters," he says. "As a result, no one worried about these things not happening. They did, and it turned out to be a special time in the broadcast history of Hawkeye athletics."

In 2018, Gary celebrated his 22nd year as the voice of the Iowa Hawkeyes.

•

After graduating from Iowa State University, Jim Knuth, Sr. Vice President at Farm Credit Services of America, worked at University Bank and Trust in Ames as a personal banker. For 12 years, he grabbed the lunch pail each day representing banks in Ames, Waterloo, and Des Moines.

The Knuth family (L to R) with Karl and Taylor (Knuth) Peterson; Jay, Taryn, Jim, Tory and Dawn.

"I started at the bottom of the depth chart and just kept working my way up," he reminisces.

In 1996, he got his big break when he joined the Farm Credit Services of the Midlands (now Farm Credit Services of America) team as a commercial agribusiness loan officer.

"Actually, when Farm Credit first called about the position, I really didn't want to interview as I didn't want to move to Omaha," Jim says. "But I had three children and was motivated to support my family. I remember going to Omaha for the job interview; they told me they were interviewing so many different candidates and I remember coming home and throwing the stuff away saying, 'I'll never get that job.'

"They called me several weeks later to tell me I was a finalist."

Then the day arrived for the second interview.

"They asked me why I thought I'd be successful in this job," Jim recalls.

"I replied, 'I've never failed at anything in my life and I don't intend to start to now.' Perhaps it was a statement of belief. Later, the person who led the interview told me, 'You got the job because of that answer.' They wanted someone with confidence."

•

"Being a leader means being a good teacher and being honest, whether it's to my children or my players. It's about being consistent all the time so they see the same thing in you each day and know what to expect depending on their actions. For every action there's a reaction and it could be positive or negative. Consistency matters to your children or your players; that way, they know what to expect and won't be flustered by an outcome."

JONATHAN HAYES, IOWA HAWKEYE TIGHT END (1981-'84)
AND FORMER CINCINNATI BENGALS ASSISTANT COACH

•

Strong character is critical to getting where you want to go.

"What's encouraging is that character can be developed," says Des Moines University President Angela Walker Franklin. "And that's good because character is about consistency. It's your core and central to who you are as an individual.

Sure, upbringing is important, says Franklin, a South Carolinian native and first woman president at DMU.

"I was taught as a child that you treat everyone the way you want to be treated. I took it to heart, always mindful of the other person and being respectful of others."

Unfortunately, culture is coarsening. Whatever the reason, people seem to be increasingly short tempered and impatient. We are less likely to give someone the benefit of the doubt. We too often assume the worst in each other and a situation. It seems the end is all that matters, never mind the means.

"It's amazing to see what's happening in the world today...the manner in which people are disrespectful, demeaning or attacking to others," Franklin says. "I'm perplexed as to how you can lose your character as you move along in life and how we get out of this challenging environment we're in as a society.

Dr. Angela Walker Franklin and her husband, Thaddeus, at Des Moines University holiday gala.

"But there's hope because character can be developed," she says. *"Character to me is everything. It's who you are and how you treat others.* Character determines how respectful you are. This is an essential ingredient."

Franklin says character starts with fundamental core values of integrity, treating others with respect and kindness. It's about getting back to the golden rule and treating others the way that you want and expect to be treated.

"If we start there, a lot of the other matters take care of themselves."

Being open to opposing views is also critical, Franklin says. How you respond to others goes a long way toward maintaining peace and increasing the likelihood that progress can be made on critical issues and projects.

"Leaders value all messages and opinions, provided they are respectful," Franklin says. "I value everyone and what they can bring to our university, to conversations, to problem solving. I only ask others for the same benefit of doubt. *If we begin respecting everyone, we will elevate the tone and tenor of the dialogue and have greater respect for our fellow humanity. Deep down in our soul, we are first and foremost human beings.*

"We all bleed the same."

Franklin says every conversation and interaction should begin with recognizing one another's humanity.

"That's particularly important when we disagree; it enables one to do so respectfully," she says. "It should not vary and depend on the moment or situation. Character, after all, is what you do and who you are when no one is looking. Be authentic. Be who you are. Don't change. Don't be one way with one person and another with someone else.

"Good character is about being consistent, understanding, and respectful of everyone, even those with which you may disagree."

•

"There's a tendency to try to hide losses or problems. But the best thing you can do is be honest with people and hope they react to the information that way, are appreciative of it and maintain a relationship. There are many things you can't control. But you can control how you deal with problems, difficulties, and circumstances. When you face adversity, don't ignore the problems and the troubles. Fight through it. It's at those times that you can either feel sorry for yourself or you can try to do the right thing. Do the right thing."

BRUCE RASTETTER, ENTREPRENEUR, HUBBARD, IOWA

•

MAKE DECISIONS

Kirk Tyler of Atlantic, Iowa-based Atlantic Bottling Company says a failure to make timely decisions is the downfall of most would-be leaders.

One would think in this day of endless data that decision making would be easy. It's not.

In fact, Tyler says leaders must avoid becoming paralyzed by too many facts and figures.

The early years of Atlantic Bottling Company – Jim Tyler, Kirk's father (left) with Sparkle, the horse pulling a wagon of iced bottles of Coca-Cola. Jim's grandfather, Frank "Perk" Tyler founded the company in 1909.

"With all the information available, it's tempting to over-study and delay acting," Tyler says. "Don't. Right or wrong, make a decision. People are asking us if we should do this or do that or what color the walls should be. At the end of the day, make a decision and move on. There are too many other things to worry about than to just stand still and keep looking at data while wondering what or if."

Data can suppress action. It can also make leaders averse to taking risks. That can be harmful, especially when you're trusted to protect and grow the world's most recognizable brand (and second-most recognizable symbol: the beveled, hour-glass-shaped Coca-Cola bottle is second only to the cross "So we're in pretty good company," says Tyler with a smile).

An aversion to taking chances and charting new territory is like quicksand for people and companies who want to go places.

"We've been around long enough to know if something is just a dumb idea. But we also have a history of saying, 'If an idea has a chance, let's try it and, if it doesn't work, we can change course if needed,'" Tyler says.

To make his point, he's quick to reference Fanta Pineapple, a product of the Coca-Cola family.

"I remember team members talking about Fanta Pineapple and that we should offer it," Tyler recalls. "I mean, really? Fanta Pineapple? Everyone around here looks like you and me. But some thought that our growing Hispanic community would enjoy the product. It was worth a try. So we did. Low and behold, today we're selling the heck out of it.

"I admitted to the team that I was wrong on that one," Kirk adds, "and they've never let me forget it!"

•

Don't get comfortable. That's the advice of University of Iowa President Bruce Harreld.

Choose a different course. Go someplace where you won't be comfortable. Stand up when the going gets rough.

"When something goes wrong, does the person closest to the fire run into it or away from it?" he asks.

It's impossible to say why some flee and others come in for a closer look. But it's the latter, Harreld says, that's a distinguishing characteristic of leaders.

"Those who care most and set an example for others want to confront challenges," says Harreld, who faced a bitter confirmation process prior to being selected in the fall of 2015 as the university's 21st president. "When some people see a problem, they may try to sound bite it, spin it, paper over it or turn away from it. But that doesn't solve it. And it certainly doesn't earn the respect of others or give them the skills and credibility to take their game to the next level."

People who avoid struggles, challenges, taking the narrow path, or veering from conventional wisdom don't get the experience required to be effective leaders. Soon, employees, members, or constituents start to think you're more interested in ducking or dodging than calling a spade a spade.

Indecision, says Harreld, demonstrates an inability to pick your course and stick to it.

"What on Earth would make people want to follow that kind of leader?" he asks.

"Now you could take almost any issue you see reported on CNN the past several years in the context of how we as a country are dealing with them," Harreld says. "For example, people who do violent things with firearms. We tend to have a 'this-or-that' conversation – like 'Should we ban certain weapons or have more mental health support? Or should we arm teachers or redesign buildings?'

"For many, it's this or that, one or the other when, in fact, the answer is both."

Harreld readily admits he doesn't have the solution for every complicated problem.

"What I do know is that we have to stop looking for simple answers to complex problems. We have to start learning that the best answers could be a little bit of this or a little bit of that.

"Rather than always debate, we should try some things and see what we learn and try a few other things and see what we learn. Over time, we can evaluate and improve.

"Leaders get things right by incorporating the best of every idea."

•

Shooting straight also means being honest and loyal, says Scott Raecker.

Unfortunately, loyalty is becoming a lost part of character building and this manifests itself in many ways.

The Raeckers attending No. 1 Iowa vs No. 2 Michigan (1985) in Kinnick. It was the first time in more than 40 years that the top-two ranked college football teams met during the regular season. Iowa was victorious 12-10 thanks to a field goal booted by kicker Rob Houghtlin as regulation time expired.

Raecker, who serves as executive director of The Robert D. and Billie Ray Center, Drake University, says, "People shouldn't stay in bad places or bad jobs. But there seems to be too much of 'what's in it for me' and not seeing the greater good or making the best out of bad situations."

The Waterloo native and former state legislator says a good example of loyalty exemplified is Drake University Women's Basketball Coach Jennie Baranczyk.

"What Coach Jennie has done is quite amazing, above and beyond the winning," says Raecker about the Dowling High School grad who was named to Drake Women's Basketball's top post in 2012.

"She's brought together a group of young women who have expectations and knowledge that they are playing for something greater than themselves," Reacker explains. "She plays ten players and no one can hang with them in the 4th period because everyone else is gassed and no longer has fresh legs.

"She's taking kids who were the best players on their high school teams and gotten them to buy in and believe it's better for them to play 20 minutes but be on a championship team than be a 40-minute starter with a big stat sheet and finish middle of the pack in the league."

This was manifested, says Raecker, when the most valuable player in the 2017 Missouri Valley women's basketball conference tournament was a reserve from Drake.

"There's something to be said about the importance of loyalty, whether to a team, system or each other," Raecker says. "The results are often optimal for both the individual and group."

REFLECTIONS

Who do you need to have an honest conversation with to resolve a lingering issue, solve a problem or reach new goals?

_____

_____

_____

_____

How will you approach them? When?

_____

_____

_____

_____

What is the one habit you should start? Quit? How will you achieve success? When?

_____

_____

_____

_____

3 Live with Passion

"Positive attitude and positive effort are 90 percent of everything we do in life," says Jim Knuth, Sr. Vice President with Farm Credit Services of America.

To have "zest" is to have great enthusiasm and energy. And, just like a smile, it can be infectious.

When you're around someone who has a passion for what they do, your spirits are lifted. Everyone's game is elevated when a leader brings energy to a conversation, meeting, room, board, job, hobby, or relationship.

Having "zest" or passion for what you do and who you serve is an important key to success.

Contrast passion with just going through the motions—doing only what's required. Which is more inspiring? Which will rally others to your side, to your cause, to victory?

Leaders are the fuel that ignites accomplishment. Live with passion and others will gravitate toward you, doors will open, opportunities will arise, and you'll be fulfilled.

Just ask Terry Branstad. Nominated by President Donald Trump in early 2017 and confirmed by the U.S. Senate in May 2017 as U.S. Ambassador to China, the farm boy from Winnebago County holds the distinction of being America's youngest and longest serving governor.

"When I think about success, the first ingredient that comes to mind is having a positive attitude and real passion for what you do," Branstad says.

Terry Branstad was raised near Leland, Iowa, and serves as the U.S. Ambassador to China. He is widely regarded as a tireless worker and positive and passionate about issues he cares about. Branstad holds the distinction of being both Iowa's youngest and longest-serving governor. He has never lost an election (photo by Joseph L. Murphy)

"When you have setbacks in your life, you can't let them defeat you. A passion for work and life is a tremendous asset when setbacks happen. And they will."

Some of the most successful people in history, like Abraham Lincoln, had what it took to lead their countries back from some of the worst times possible, says Branstad, who took up residence with his family in Beijing in June 2017.

"Through it all, [Lincoln] had the vision to create the transcontinental railroad that tied the country together east and west—a rail line eventually completed four years after his assassination."

Branstad attended the University of Iowa where he earned his undergraduate degree before serving in the U.S. Army and obtaining a law degree from Drake University. He was inspired to attend Iowa, he says, largely because of the accomplishments of Forest City-native Herb Thompson, who led his high school to runner up in the 1949 state basketball tournament.

"He then went on to play for the University of Iowa. So when I was a little kid, I'd listen to the Iowa men's basketball broadcasts on WHO Radio because this guy from my home town was playing for them."

But that wasn't the only "Thompson" the governor admired. "I was a big fan of Gary Thompson and his play for Roland and Iowa State University," he says with a smile. "He's another hero for our state and small towns. Gary had a profound passion for his community, our state, business and the game of basketball.

"He just loved where he was from and what he did. All great leaders do."

When Branstad thinks of leaders with drive and passion, he also references Churchill.

"He warned about Hitler and the dangers of appeasement and was largely ignored until the Germans had virtually occupied most of continental Europe. Then, they turned to him to be prime minister and lead Great Britain back from the threshold of destruction."

Churchill, he says, possessed the courage and tenacity to inspire the British people to never give up and to fight for what they believed.

"I don't remember all of his quotes but one of my favorites is, 'We shall defend our island, whatever the cost may be, we shall fight on the beaches, we shall fight on the landing grounds, we shall fight in the fields and in the streets, we shall fight in the hills; we shall never surrender.'"

•

FORTY YEARS A BLUR

"It wasn't a job for me, even though it was seven days a week and a lot of hours," says retired Iowa assistant athletic trainer John Streif.

His passion is what motivated him to excel in the role for 40 years.

"It's just what I did. But it wasn't a job. When people ask how many hours I put in and why I did that, I just reply that you wouldn't do it if you didn't have a passion for it, didn't enjoy it and if it wasn't right for you. So looking back over a 40-year career, serving in that role must have been right for me. I'm just fortunate it lasted as long as it did."

For John, one of the most rewarding aspects of his career was seeing young people come into the university setting and learn and grow.

"There are always problems and to help them grow through those problems—whether it be family issues back home or girlfriend problems or alcohol or drugs—is special," says Streif who retired from the university in 2012.

"Iowa is no different than Iowa State, UNI, Drake or any other school, and these young people are no different than the young people at other schools or in other walks of life," Streif says. "To be there with young people during their medical issues—like a young man or woman who comes to campus and they have to go through their first surgeries and their families are somewhere else—I always tried to be there for those people and to share with them.

John Streif

"To see that growth over four to five years they are here, there can't be anything more rewarding in sports."

•

"Leadership is about people," says Jim Knuth, Sr. Vice President for Farm Credit Services of America.

"You manage tasks and things. But leadership always come down to people. You lead people."

Jim's perspective is anchored in personal experience. He was raised on a grain and cattle farm near Rhodes, Iowa, and was a big-time, small-town high school athlete excelling in basketball, track, baseball and football.

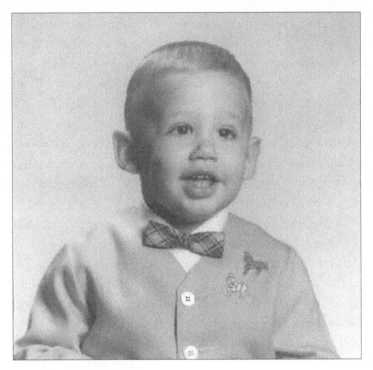

Jim Knuth – just a baby (1962).

His high school football coach was Gary Swenson, a 1993 Iowa Football Coaches Hall of Fame inductee who now serves as head coach of the West Des Moines Valley High School Tigers.

Jim admits that his success in athletics was largely unexpected. "Not growing up in an athletic family meant I could evolve in sports without expectations. It really didn't cross my mind that participating in high school sports would lead to something after high school until I began receiving letters of interest from college programs."

He credits Coach Swenson "for really being the first coach who believed in me. He recognized my potential, my talent and my work ethic.

"I was kid from a little small town and there was no such thing as ESPN so it was difficult to put context around what I could be," says Jim. "Without his belief in me, I doubt I would have ever gone to Iowa State University."

But a good leader, says Jim, fosters belief in those they work with. And when he arrived in Ames to play ball for the Cyclones, it was wide receivers coach Mack Brown who greeted him, supported his development as an athlete, and encouraged him to develop as a Big-8 football player. That experience lives with Jim today and he applies it in his role at Farm Credit.

"There are many similarities between sports and business, including the selection and hiring of a team," he says. "You identify members of the team. You recruit them. You develop them. You encourage and support them. You challenge them. You inspire them. Eventually, the sum is always greater than the parts.

"The key is finding the most talented and engaged people. There's no substitute for either one. Both are equally important.

"If you have mediocre talent, you'll have a mediocre team," Knuth says. "The same can be said for hiring someone who is talented but not engaged. *Engagement is everything. It means they've given you their head and their heart. If you give your heart to something—what you choose to wake up early to get at it—that means you're engaged. This makes all the difference. There's no substitute for talent and engagement.*"

•

Having a passion for life and all its twists and turns doesn't just happen. It's the result of a series of connections, beginning with having sound character.

Central to that is possessing faith and exhibiting love, says Scott Raecker, a former Iowa state legislator who serves as executive director of The Robert D. and Billie Ray Center.

"Love is a very powerful thing and essential to leadership and character. Love is not a soft skill," Raecker says. "I'm not talking about the emotion, romantic sense of the word. I'm talking about loving what you do in life. About loving people who don't think like you do. Loving those moments that come along in life—like writing a book about Chuck Long or visiting with people to capture their perspective about leadership."

A graduate of Grinnell College (BA Political Science and Religious Studies), Raecker says everyone would be better served—and the country, too—if more people would demonstrate love a little bit better.

"You do that by serving others. And you must do so with character. It fulfills purpose and being when you get up each day trying to make a difference in someone else's life.

"Love. Love life. Love what you do. Love simple things," Raecker says. "Love complex things. Love your family. Love friends. Love people. All people. The essence of life is love, and when we can demonstrate this in our work, it has dramatic impact on others as well as ourselves. For me, passion for a cause greater than self is the fuel for love."

Scott Raecker (far left) helps cut the ribbon celebrating the opening of The Robert D. and Billie Ray Center at Drake University (2017). The event doubled as a celebration of Gov. Robert D. Ray (front, left), with guests enjoying his favorite flavor of ice cream (peppermint) and a large batch of chocolate chip cookies. Ray, a mentor of Scott's, passed July 8, 2018 at the age of 89.

Leaders also have a positive outlook, says Iowa State University President Wendy Wintersteen.

"So even when something goes bad, you can't start feeling sorry for yourself or lamenting the situation you're in. That only leads to negative thoughts and feelings. And those negative thoughts become predictors of the future. If you get overly negative or feel sorry for yourself, then you predict a future that looks like that."

Wintersteen, appointed ISU president in 2017, says those who keep a positive outlook have an advantage over those who get caught up in a negative mindset.

"If you can say to yourself 'These are the things I'm working to achieve and I'm doing it in a way that's positive and doing it in a way that doesn't bring any negative impact to anybody else,' then you're going to keep things in perspective when things don't go right," she says. "Because everybody has bad things happen to them, or setbacks, and some of them can be very personal and some of them very difficult to deal with them. You can quickly get into self-pity or a fear-based mindset and that simply isn't the place to be.

"You must sit down and make a plan that outlines how you're going to proceed, especially during times of distress," Wintersteen says. "You're much more likely to do this if you start from a positive place."

•

WINNING FORMULA

"What am I looking for in a kid that wants to play football at Iowa? The same things we were looking for in those 1980 and 1981 seasons that were the start of a successful formula," says Iowa football head coach Kirk Ferentz.

"You think about a kid like Chuck Long and others that have come into this program—the walk-on receivers who played so well, the guys who were linemen who weren't recruited by many people but turned out to be really good football players. Sure, we've had an occasional guy that comes in polished and makes an instant impact—John Alt was one of those guys—or a Joe Hilgenberg who played center and was one of the most awesome players I've ever coached. So you learn from how kids grow and develop in a program.

"And as you do, you understand that a big ingredient in the formula is getting guys who have the requisite ability but also have a high level of pride and a great deal of passion, determination and work ethic and are team players.

"Those attributes are critical," says the dean of Big Ten football coaches, "not just at Iowa but to be successful in life."

•

John Quinn is a passionate motivator as Chief of Police for Waukee, Iowa, a bustling suburb of Des Moines.

A graduate of Dowling Catholic High School in West Des Moines, Quinn played quarterback at Iowa State University (including his freshman and sophomore year for legendary coach Earl Bruce) before earning an accounting degree.

Iowa State University quarterback John Quinn in the open field.

The youngest of five children, John learned responsibility at an early age. His dad played college football at Miami of Ohio, was a fighter pilot in World War II, practiced law, and had a long and successful career in the U.S. Federal Bureau of Investigation and Pentagon.

When John was 12, the family moved to Des Moines.

"Dad thought the town was a good place to raise a family," he recalls.

As a boy, John was extremely quiet and enjoyed playing sports. Football quickly became his favorite.

"Dad, having played quarterback as a youth, taught me how to throw a football. I thought I was pretty handy at it."

One particular practice made an indelible impression on the young man.

"So it's the second day of practice at Dowling and coaches are rotating players through different positions. As was the case back then, practices were very disciplined. Quarterbacks would throw, receivers would catch. After a set of drills, footballs would be collected, brought back to the quarterback and placed at their feet to throw again.

"Well, I had been getting frustrated during practice at the number of poorly thrown balls and dropped passes. So, after yet another dropped ball, out of frustration, I picked up the football and threw it back to the quarterback. I mean I sailed it. The football hit him squarely in the nose and broke it. The coach wheeled around and asked who threw it. By this time, I'm already balling. I fess up to it and prepared to take the consequences, including getting kicked off the team.

"Instead, the coach says, 'Quinn, you're quarterback. Now get in line.'"

It was a long walk home that night for Quinn as he prepared to face the wrath of his father.

"I recall coming home that night after practice. My dad asked how I did at practice. I told him I was named starting quarterback."

"'I wondered how long it would take 'em,'" he replied.

•

"Sometimes it's difficult to understand the common thread running through the experiences I've had," admits University of Iowa Bruce Harreld.

You can't blame him for arriving at such an assessment.

Harreld, named to the post in 2015 with more than a hint of controversy, taught at Northwestern University and Harvard Business School, held senior positions at Kraft Foods and Boston Market, and answered the call from Lou Gerstner to come to IBM to help it avoid bankruptcy.

The latter, Harreld admits, was the toughest challenge he's ever undertaken.

"The company was in a really troubled financial state—there were riots and threats of physical violence."

Yet when asked to find the commonality in all of them, Harreld points to his interest in accumulating experiences and being eager to "learn about things."

Challenges, he says, aren't to be downplayed or avoided. True leaders embrace them.

"I'd see something that was a challenge and would be interested in solving it. Clearly, IBM was a challenge at the time. The bigger the problem, the more interested I was in it. *I'm passionate about solving problems. Be passionate about that, too, because the world needs problem solvers.*"

Passion is what drives leaders to and through challenging situations.

Are you willing to take the reins when the going gets tough?

Are you passionate enough?

LIVE, WORK AND DAIRY WITH PASSION!

Passion can separate you from the competition.

Just ask Miriam Erickson Brown, CEO of AE Dairy.

The year was 1930 and the Great Depression was taking hold of America.

What a perfect time to launch a dairy business!

Well, in retrospect, perhaps not. But that's exactly what happened.

Today, that company is preparing to celebrate its 90th birthday!

Warren Erickson, Miriam Erickson Brown, Jim Erickson

AE Dairy, a Des Moines, Iowa landmark known and loved for its fresh, delicious dairy products (and the tulips and bigger-than-life cows named Annie and Eric that adorn its beautiful campus adjacent University Avenue on the east side of Des Moines), was founded in 1930 by Miriam's grandfather, Iver Erickson.

The dairy competition at the time was fierce. There were 150 dairies with operating permits in Des Moines.

But Iver and his family moved ahead, undeterred.

Since 1930, the company has immersed itself in all things dairy. "Because dairy products have a way of bringing people together!" says Miriam with an infectious smile and genuine passion and conviction.

When it comes to passion, AE's is creating great-tasting dairy in flavors that people love, because it thinks dairy products should not only be part of a healthy diet — they should taste incredible, too.

And they do!

From milks, lemonade and yogurts (lemon mousse, strawberry rhubarb pie and peach cobbler – can you say "yum?!") to cottage cheese and sour cream, the company is unyielding in its focus on quality. It's one of the reasons it continues the tradition started in 1930 of taste-testing every product it makes every week.

Miriam says the company constantly challenges itself to be the best at dairying.

"Everything we do is all about great taste, so we do lots of tasting and testing before we introduce new flavors. Sometimes it takes months or years to get a flavor just right," she says.

All its milk comes from Iowa family farms, and all AE products are made in Des Moines, arriving in stores within hours of being produced.

"We aren't the biggest dairy out there," Miriam adds, "but we don't want to be. We just want our customers to be delighted. And we've got lots of ideas and are already working on creating the next, best thing."

•

What you are doing to delight your customers? What are you working on right now that will be the next, best thing?

Live and work with passion. Be relentless in your pursuit of quality. It works for AE. It will work for you, too.

REFLECTIONS

List three things that you're passionate about?

_____

_____

_____

_____

What brings you inspiration and fulfillment?

_____

_____

_____

_____

How can you do more of those things?

_____

_____

_____

_____

4 Be Ready

What do you do when circumstances turn against you? Or when little is expected of you?

Do you cut corners? Do you coast? Do you fold? Give up?

A defeatist attitude insulates you from the readiness required to act on opportunity—to break through with an idea that can improve your business, help the team accomplish a shared goal, or provide a boost for a charity or non-profit struggling to survive.

Time away from the office, from a project, from responsibility, is important.

But just like grilling a hamburger over an open flame (a favorite pastime of mine by the way!), you can easily overcook it when it comes to having downtime.

Being satisfied can become habit forming. Being a leader involves physics. As the saying goes, "a body at rest tends to stay at rest while a body in motion tends to stay in motion."

John Campbell, long-time KCRG-TV sports director who covered more Iowa Hawkeye football, basketball, and press conferences than he can count, relished being in motion. He says you need a lot of drive to be successful, regardless of the profession.

"You want to do as good as you can in getting the details and taking responsibility for your work. As a reporter, that's especially true because your name is attached to the story for everyone to see. You better be right."

Preparation was a big part of showing up to work ready to do the job and do it well, says John Campbell (right), retired KCRG-TV (Cedar Rapids) sports director pictured here with Iowa Hawkeyes' football coach Hayden Fry following a win over Penn State in Happy Valley.

Being ready means building relationships and keeping them, adds Kirk Tyler, CEO and Chairman of Atlantic Bottling Company.

The visionary and leader of a company, who does business in several states including Iowa, Illinois, Wisconsin, Minnesota, and Missouri, says he learned the importance of making connections by observing his grandfather and father.

They made it a point, he says, to get to know, on a very personal level, the various owners and presidents of companies they did business with, and their employees, too.

"They were always ready to meet someone and figure out ways to learn and improve."

Kirk says the company strives to be different by first thinking about what's best for its employees.

"When we do, we know we'll do what's best for our business, and that always keeps you on your toes."

Some people ask Kirk why the company backed by nearly 800 employees transitioned in 2016 from a relatively small and comfortable business office and distribution center in Waukee, Iowa to a spacious facility on the south side of Iowa's capitol city.

"Folks asked why we needed a building this big and why we were expanding so much," Kirk recalls.

"The answer was simple. We weren't thinking about the next month, or next quarter, or even next year. We were doing what was best for our employees for the next generation. It wasn't an easy one, but it was guided by how we had previously managed opportunities for growth.

Tyler says it would have been easy for his father, who's now in his 90s, to have said when considering the opportunity, 'You know what, we're comfortable right now and doing a pretty good job; things are OK; let's not take this leap of faith and that much new territory by almost doubling our footprint.'

"There's an aversion to taking chances and charting new territory," says Kirk Tyler, CEO and Chairman of Atlantic Bottling Company pictured here in 1986 during a visit to Hong Kong. "We have a history of saying, 'If an idea has a chance, let's try it.'"

"But that wasn't an answer. So we talked a lot about the pros and cons. We changed our mind three times a day. I asked him a lot of questions to take advantage of his perspective and experience.

"And then it finally dawned on me," Kirk says resolutely, leaning forward with hands folded on the table. "I said, 'Dad, if you and grandpa wouldn't have taken a leap of faith and had the foresight to buy the Des Moines franchise in the 1970s, we probably wouldn't be in business.' So is it fair to the next generation of our family and employees to deny the opportunity that comes with growth? Of course not.

"And it's in that context that we make decisions that move this company forward in a way that's positive for everyone involved."

Few experiences can better hone one's ability to make decisions than serving in the military.

Just ask Bob Myers, the long-time CEO of Casey's General Store.

"You can just go chapter and verse on all the many lessons the military bestowed on me," he says. "It prepared me for senior leadership. To be ready. To be at the top of my game. It's all about leading others and at times, in difficult situations."

He says that leadership is something a person learns through experiences—through preparation and training and from being ready to do the task that needs to be done in the moment.

"Leadership is not the kind of thing you can learn in the classroom," he says. "You learn different models of leadership and the principles of good leadership – but you learn it best on the job and with good mentorship guiding you along the way. You also pick it up after you make mistakes and correcting your errors and going on and learning more – that's what leadership is about."

•

Gary Dolphin, veteran Iowa Hawkeye broadcaster, says his break in the profession came in 1989 with a ring of the telephone.

He's glad he answered the phone, because on the other end of the line was a friend who had gained All-American honors as a cross country runner at Loras College while Gary was serving as a TV reporter in Dubuque.

Now the associate athletic director at Northwestern College in Evanston, IL, Gary's friend informed him that the school was in need of a play-by-play announcer for men's basketball.

"So he called and said, 'Gary, I thought of you. Now, I know it's quite a drive for you from Dubuque to Chicago but I wanted to offer the job to you first. If you don't want it, I get it. No hard feelings and I'll move on.'"

Gary immediately interrupted.

"I'd love the opportunity to try to get back into the Big Ten," he said.

Gary had broadcast Iowa sports in Dubuque for five years in the 1970s. The opportunity to get back into the Big Ten by taking the gig at Northwestern was too good to pass up.

"That was 1989. And so, I did. Six years later, the Iowa job surprisingly opens when the powers-to-be make a change with their broadcast crew," Gary recalls. "I mean, who knew? After all, everyone figured that (Jim) Zabel and (Bob) Brooks and (Ron) Gonder would be there forever.

"Goes to show it pays to be ready to answer an opportunity when it comes knocking. Even if it may not be the ultimate summit you desire, it could very well be a step forward in the direction you're wanting to travel."

And his readiness gave him the confidence to take the leap when the opportunity arose.

Being open to opportunity is an important leadership quality, says Iowa State University's president.

"Maybe it's being invited to run for an elected office on student government or to serve on a team or committee," says Dr. Wendy Wintersteen. "When the invitation is made, listen carefully to what that opportunity is and if it's a door that may be opening.

"Then, be brave enough to take the time to say, 'You know, I'm going to take advantage of that opportunity. I'm going to move forward. I know it's going to require extra effort but I'm going to take advantage of the opportunity that's being presented to me.'"

Perhaps it's a new or different experience that you never thought you would do but someone else thinks you should consider it.

"If you can be disciplined to not only listen but carefully consider different opportunities, well, that's how you begin to shape your future and achieve new goals," Wintersteen says.

"Every step of my journey as an undergraduate was on the path that I wanted to take to be a field crop agronomist. That's what I wanted to do. Then I took an interest in entomology to broaden out my education.

Wendy Wintersteen teaching at an Iowa State University Extension field day for farmers.

"By the time I earned my graduate degree and Ph.D. in entomology, I knew I was going to do something different, and that I was going to be in a much more focused area. It really is about carefully considering choices, not shying away from opportunity, and trying new things.

"True success comes from acting on doors that are opened to you. Be ready to step through them when they do."

•

Letting your guard down is a recipe for disaster.

"I always tell my team that it's the little detail that will bring you to your knees," says Randy Edeker, Chairman, CEO and President of Hy-Vee. "You always have to be ready. Always."

To make his point, Randy shares a story about the time Hy-Vee sponsored a world-recognized triathlon – an event Randy played a key role in creating.

"Ric (Jurgens), who was Hy-Vee's chairman and CEO at the time, came to me one night as he was prone to do—at 5:30 p.m. or something like that. I'll never forget it because when Ric had a job for me, he called me 'buddy boy.'

"And on this particular night, he came to me and said, 'Buddy boy, I know you have enough to do, but I want you to work on something. I want us to explore putting on a triathlon. I want to drive our health and wellness brand and a triathlon would be the perfect way to do it.'"

Randy Edeker (left) with Iowa Gov. Terry Branstad for signing of the Helpful Smile Proclamation (2014).

Randy immediately went to work to make Ric's vision a reality. And it was a hit.

Soon, Randy began handing the reigns to others.

"As I phased out of it in the fourth year, I was turning it over to other people. And we had an NBC broadcast that we did. I remember recalling that it would be the little things that bring us to our knees because we had all of the big things covered—the grandstands and the jumbotrons.

"And there we were, at the finish line, the race is done, a $200,000 prize is about to be awarded as part of a $1 million payout—the biggest in the world in the sport. The NBC cameras are on and we're about to present the ceremonial check to the winner… and we don't have a magic marker to fill out the check! Not one. Right? So we're going through glove compartments of cars and turning the place inside out for a magic marker that probably retailed for about 75 cents.

"To this day, we remember and all talk about that afternoon and the importance of being prepared, about how much the little things matter."

Do your homework

"Experience, confidence and preparation. They've been invaluable," says Gary Dolphin. "My time with Northwestern gave me a lot of confidence, as did my tenure with the Chicago Bears. Both got me up to speed with the industry and what it expects out of you. So I was very confident in my ability when Iowa called.

"What also helped me is that I understood how big the Iowa job was. I'm not from New York. I wasn't coming in from California or Ohio. I fully understood the passion that people had in Iowa for the University of Iowa. And I tried to treat it just as I would have back in my early days with KDTH Radio. You're really just talking into a microphone. I never visualized that I'm staring at 150,000 people who tune in at any one time. Doing so would be intimidating."

Preparation is key to success, regardless of the profession or pursuit.

"I always do my homework. I've benefited from the ability to look at a bunch of notes, and not only glean what's important out of those notes for that particular game, but retain it…although the retention isn't nearly as good as it used to be," Dolphin says with a laugh.

With preparation comes confidence, an essential ingredient for success.

"You have to be confident in your ability. Not cocky, but appreciative that you have a job and trust your own instincts," Dolphin says. "You then must prepare by doing your homework.

"What really helped me is that I knew Bob Brooks and I knew Jim Zabel and Ron Gonder and they knew me and understood how I did things. Certainly, none of them were overjoyed that they were being told to step aside. But they knew that they were in my position at one time and they were very professional about it.

"Well, maybe everyone but Jim," Dolphin adds with a good-natured chuckle.

MILK MAN

Gene Meyer—community leader, board president, fundraiser, mayor, dad, and volunteer—has a knack for opening the door when opportunity knocks.

Perhaps it's because he started out knocking on doors in Jesup, Iowa, early each morning as a young man.

His first job was building houses as a member of his father's construction crew. When he turned 13, his father declared one evening over supper that Gene was working hard enough to earn a paycheck. So, for the next two years, he earned money constructing homes and baling hay and straw on his uncle's farm.

Then, out of nowhere, unspeakable tragedy struck. His 47-year-old father died suddenly of a heart attack. Gene, just 15 years of age, was quickly tasked with new responsibilities, not the least of which was finding new employment.

"For the first time I had to go to work for someone who wasn't an immediate family member or relative," Gene recalls. "So, I landed a milk job for Carnation Dairy. I would get up every morning at 4 a.m. so I could be working by 5."

First on the to-do list was delivering milk and juice to the front door steps of the people in Jesup. Then, he would help stock the shelves at the community's two grocery stores.

In addition to managing adversity, Gene learned how to make good use of his time and the value of being productive.

Because it was a small town, he was also able to speak directly to the person running Carnation Dairy. Gene would inquire about the details of running a business, from profit margins and working with suppliers to developing distribution networks and how best to price assorted products depending on the buyer. It was his first introduction to economics.

Gene attended a local community college and earned a degree in police science, landing a job in public safety as a part-time communication dispatcher for the Iowa State Patrol in Cedar Rapids. At age 19, he moved to Fairfield, Iowa, where he worked for a state patrol communications center. He also attended Parsons College in Fairfield, which, at the time, had one of just a few four-year criminal justice programs in the state.

Gene Meyer playing on his first set of drums at his home in Jesup, Iowa in 1964.

Following graduation, he took a job as a state patrol officer. Just 10 weeks into the academy, Iowa's criminal investigation bureau offered Gene employment as a special agent.

"So I hung up the uniform before I ever put it on in favor of a suit and tie and went to work at the state Department of Criminal Investigation," Gene recalls.

He would eventually serve 37 years in the department, retiring as its director.

Gene's extensive political and professional connections landed him on the West Des Moines Community Schools Board of Education, serving nine years total and six as president. He was elected Mayor of West Des Moines and was relishing a third four-year term when Iowa Gov. Chet Culver tabbed him as Iowa Department of Public Safety commissioner.

Gene Meyer, President of the Greater Des Moines Partnership

It was a job Gene didn't think he wanted.

"I was flattered at the offer but after a lot of thought and soul-searching, I concluded that the commissioner's job wasn't the right one for me," Gene recalls. "I was really enjoying being mayor and looking forward to a third term."

So, he typed a formal letter to the governor-elect explaining his decision.

"I had the letter in hand the next morning at 7 a.m. as my wife Kathy and I drove to Stillwell Junior High in West Des Moines where she was a teacher," Gene recalls. "She asked what I was going to do and I told her that I was going to refuse the job. She asked if I was going to mail it and I said I didn't know.

"So we say goodbye and as I'm leaving Stillwell, my phone rings and it's Mike Blouin who was living and working in Dubuque.

"And Blouin, who had come up short to Culver during the Democratic primary for governor, was now on the inside and knew in advance many of the governor-elect's picks. He says, 'Hey, congratulations Gene. I understand Chet is going to tab you as his commissioner of public safety.'

"And I reply, 'Well, Michael, I'm not so sure I'm going to take the job.' And quite frankly, that's all he needed to hear as he proceeded to chew my backside. 'What Gene? You've been mayor, you've done this and you've done that. But Gene, have you ever been asked to serve in a governor's cabinet?' I said, 'No.' He replied, 'You do this.'

"So I shredded the letter, called Chet and said, 'I'm in,'" Gene added. "Resigning as Mayor of West Des Moines was one of the toughest decisions I've ever made. But it was the right decision.

"And that's an important life lesson. Sometimes the most impactful decisions are the most difficult. Consider the opportunities that accompany new opportunities. And be sure to seek out advice and consider the input you receive from others you trust and respect."

•

"Preparation has always been part of the process because you just never know when you can step in. You have to be ready. Be persistent. And believe in yourself. You have a team and it's family and it's about what's best for them. Those who put themselves ahead of the team hurt the team. When you align as a team, you succeed. And when you don't, you struggle."

MARK VLASIC, IOWA HAWKEYE QUARTERBACK (1982-86);
4TH ROUND NFL DRAFT PICK (1987)

•

LEADERSHIP READY

Dr. Angela L. Walker Franklin, a South Carolinian native who was raised in a family that stressed education, appreciates the journey that brought her to Des Moines, Iowa as president of Des Moines University.

"My mother was an English teacher and dad a business owner so there were expectations for success," she says. "Education was seen as 'the way' growing up in a small community so it was something my parents focused on quite a bit. There was no question about going to college and aspiring for things that were bigger and better than where we were."

But that didn't mean there wasn't trepidation. Or that the journey from small-town South Carolina to being the leader of students, faculty, and staff of a distinguished medical school located in the heart of the Midwest would be clearly marked.

Quite the opposite.

As a student entering Furman University (Travelers Rest, South Carolina), Franklin's initial plan was to study music and be a music teacher.

"I loved teaching so I thought I'd be an education major," she recalls. "But by the time I was a junior in college, psychology just kept talking to me, mainly because I had a real interest in working with special needs children. So I changed my major my junior year to be a psychology major and become a clinical psychologist."

The idea went over like a lead balloon back home.

"I remember the conversation with my father and it went something like, 'You mean to say you're going to be one of those people who others pay money to talk to them? Is that what you plan to do? Who's going to pay you money to just come and talk?'"

Undeterred, Franklin set sail to reach her goal of becoming a psychologist and therapist and working with families with children with special needs.

Dr. Angela Walker Franklin, PhD, President, Des Moines University. "Leaders bring others with them," says Franklin. "It can never be just about you."

She landed at Emory University for her doctoral work in psychology. There she did considerable work with families and went on to work with couples.

"So that was my life plan that I would become a clinical psychologist."

Franklin pauses.

"And then this opportunity – to serve as president of Des Moines University – presented itself."

It's a part of her life story that Franklin loves to tell and that can be an inspiration to others.

"I allowed myself to be open to opportunities; I sort of rode that train where it took me," she says.

With her Doctor of Philosophy (PhD) in hand from Emory College, Franklin looked to the future. But as she did, the words of her father kept returning. How was she going to build a practice? Who was going to come and pay money to talk to her? She became anxious. She had questions about her next step.

And that's when she received a phone call with an invitation to teach psychology at a medical school. It was a tempting offer. As a faculty member at a medical school, she could be the only PhD in the department that was also home to a faculty practice plan. In other words, Franklin could not only teach but also build a practice.

She decided to go for it and got the position of assistant professor of psychiatry at Morehouse School of Medicine, a relatively new school located in Atlanta. The move got Franklin into the academic realm, while simultaneously building a practice and teaching a more mature, professional group of students. For nearly twenty years, Franklin ascended the ranks, moving from assistant professor to full professor and taking on administrative work, including dean of admissions, dean of student affairs, and director of counseling services.

"It was all intriguing and getting involved on the administrative side of education was something I enjoyed more than I thought," she says. "So now, after two decades of trying new things and just going where this journey is leading me, I'm becoming perplexed, trying to figure out what I do next.

"*I'm struggling with the idea of exactly what do I want to be when I grow up!*" Franklin adds with a smile. "*I had children at the time; they*

were all thinking it was really strange that mom doesn't know yet what she wanted to do; what's wrong with this picture? Here I have a PhD and seem to be doing some things that adults do and yet I'm admitting that I don't know yet what I want to be when I grow up… This is crazy!"

That's when Franklin was encouraged by her mentors to enroll in the American Council on Education Fellowship Program. It offered Franklin and other academic professionals the opportunity to job shadow university presidents. The timing was ideal.

"I was quickly becoming a sponge, latching on to people and roles and responsibilities in areas that I admired," she recalls. "So the president of the medical school was someone I admired; some of the deans I admired; I found myself wanting to learn more and more as I advanced in my career as a member of the faculty there; and it brought along some new opportunities.

"I was open to raising my hand to volunteer on committees, and this is essential to growing as a person and a leader. These individuals took me under their wings, became my greatest supporters, and helped me expand my scope and my experiences."

As a Fellowship participant, Franklin absorbed the year-long shadowing a president of another university. The mentoring that accompanied it expanded her thinking and what she could do by combining her background and degree in clinical psychology with administrative experience.

"I just soaked it all in," she says. "It was my year of affirmation. At that moment that I knew I wanted to be a college president. Now I didn't quite know how I would get there, but I knew that was the career path I would follow."

After completing the Fellowship, Franklin took advantage of every enrichment opportunity she could. With the hard work and dedication to her profession, she assumed a variety of new leadership roles, including Associate Vice President and Vice Dean of Morehouse School of Medicine and Executive Vice President and Provost of Meharry Medical College (Nashville).

While at Meharry, her phone rang again.

"I received a phone call one day from a search firm that I had gotten to know about an opportunity in a place I had never heard of—Des Moines University—in city I had never visited—Des Moines.

"Surely they weren't interested in my background," Franklin recalls saying to herself during the interview process. "I'm very different. I'd be the first woman, the first person of color to lead the institution—one that's been around since 1898.

"I thought they would never hire me," Franklin admits.

Nonetheless, Franklin, a true leader, made herself ready for the unknown opportunities that presented themselves throughout her entire career. In March 2011, she was named the 15th president of Des Moines University.

REFLECTIONS

What can you do today that will bring unexpected joy to someone else?

_____

_____

_____

_____

_____

_____

Commit to reading two books and following three blogs pertaining to leadership in the next six months. List them here.

_____

_____

_____

_____

_____

_____

5 Own setbacks. Share Success.

True leadership means sharing the accolades and owning the disappointments and shortcomings.

Do you own yours? And, more importantly, do you celebrate success with others?

A true leader doesn't hoard praise and success. A true leader takes responsibility for setbacks. They make sure the spotlight shines brightly on those around them when success is achieved.

Doug Reichardt, retired chairman of Holmes Murphy and the Iowa Sports Foundation board gets right to the point.

"Good leaders bring others along," he says. *"As a leader, you never get to a destination by yourself."*

Bruce Rastetter, an entrepreneur from Hubbard, Iowa, agrees. "Successful people never say 'I did this' or 'I did that.' That's because no one individually can be successful," he says. "It's 'we did this' or 'we accomplished this.' Whether it's delegating or relying on someone to lean on in good times or bad times, it's a safe bet to say that no one individually has ever done great things."

Mark Vlasic knows all about team. The Iowa quarterback sat behind Chuck Long for four seasons before getting the starting nod in 1986—his final season as a college football player.

He never complained. Instead, he made sure he prepared. If he was, the team would succeed.

"As the backup quarterback, you can choose to not prepare because you're not going to take a snap or because you think the coach likes someone else better. But you have to take the approach to prepare for that specific role. You don't get as many reps on the field (as the starter) so you better spend more practice time off the field to account for that."

Leaders must be accountable, even when the tide is turning away from you, he added.

"You must shoulder the role you have, good or bad," says Mark, who played professionally for the San Diego Chargers, Kansas City Chiefs and Tampa Bay Buccaneers. "If you do that and continue to do the best you can, opportunity will come."

It did for Vlasic.

Mark Vlasic

He was the holder for the biggest field goal in Iowa football history when Rod Houghtlin booted a 29-yard kick as time expired giving No. 1 Iowa a 12-10 victory over No. 2 Michigan Oct. 19, 1985.

In his first career start to open his fifth and final season at Iowa, Mark threw for 288 yards in a 43-7 win against Iowa State University. It was also the game that, at the time, made Hayden Fry the most winningest coach in Iowa football history.

After two more victories, Mark went down with an injury. A few weeks later, he returned to the starting lineup to pitch a 93-yard touchdown pass to Quinn Early, the longest in Iowa history. He was also under center for the 1986 Holiday Bowl. Iowa was victorious 39-38 over San Diego State University. Vlasic's line: 15 of 28 passes for 222 yards, earning him MVP honors.

Taking responsibility—win or lose—is critical if you're going to be a leader and experience success, Mark says.

"That's something you really learn by playing sports. You can't say enough about the lessons and value of participating in team sports. Trusting your gut and not second guessing it, taking responsibility—it's all part of the game.

"As quarterback, you can't hold back on making a decision. If you do, you're not going to accomplish what you're trying to do. If your gut tells you this, then go with it. I believe to this day, the people I meet, the situations I get in—and I've told my kids the same thing—if it doesn't feel right, remove yourself from it. And you know when it feels right; that's when you go with it. If it's the wrong one, then learn from it and make sure you don't make the mistake again."

Those who aren't making mistakes aren't doing anything, Mark adds.

"The objective is not to repeat a mistake if you make one. Own it. Learn from it. Remember that nobody is perfect. To make the most of whatever opportunity is out there, you have to put yourself out there, too."

TAKE THE FIRE

"Chuck (Long's) time at the University of Iowa didn't start out all that great," recalls long-time KCRG-TV sports director John Campbell.

"He got the nod against Nebraska his second season and performed so poorly that he got benched the next week when they played Iowa State. They lose. So he gets the start a week later against Arizona on the road. And they win.

"From then on, it was game-on for Chuck."

Win or lose, however, Chuck always made himself available for reporters, Campbell says.

"I never wanted to let anyone down," says John Campbell, long-time sports director for KCRG-TV (Cedar Rapids). "If I was sent to cover the Hawkeyes in the Rose Bowl, I wanted to make sure I got the stories and did them well and had them back here on time. Doing good work has always meant a lot to me and is a defining character of leaders."

"That's one thing I remember about Chuck. He always made time for reporters. The other thing I recall from my years covering Hawkeye football and Chuck Long was his demeanor in those post-game interviews and how he always handled the winning and the losing.

"I mean, you'd see Coach Fry get in his face on the sidelines like he was prone to do from time to time with his quarterback. But Chuck always handled it well. Publicly, just like on the sidelines, Chuck was easy to work with. And win or lose, he showed up and answered our questions. *You gain a lot of respect for people like that – who handle the losses as professionally as they do the wins.*"

REFLECTIONS

What shortcoming can you own (either personally or as a member of a team)?

_____

_____

_____

_____

_____

_____

What two things can you do transform them into strengths?

_____

_____

_____

_____

_____

_____

6 Show up

Hayden Fry was a farm boy at heart. He knew and respected the inner strength that came from working hard. And sweating even harder.

His roots were planted firmly in the rust-colored, west Texas soil on which his family called home. He was raised on a farm and both his mother (one of seven siblings) and father came from farming backgrounds, too.

Hayden's grandpa served as a Texas Ranger who, when off duty, would set out into the countryside to lasso wild horses. On a good day, they'd fetch $5 each. Difficult work and meager earnings. But it paid the bills.

"Nobody really thought we could win," recalls University of Iowa football coach Hayden Fry (1979-98). "So I first had to establish a positive environment. That takes a tremendous amount of work. It's more than Xs and Os, although that's a big part of it. It's about instilling leadership and discipline." Fry amassed 143 victories as Iowa's head coach, second all-time to Kirk Ferentz who earned win No. 144 Sept. 1, 2018 (33-7 versus Northern Illinois). *Photo courtesy of University of Iowa Athletics Communications*

Working hard for a day's pay was reinforced in Hayden after serving a stint in the Marines. He also came to appreciate the gratification that came from giving 110 percent.

These qualities, combined with natural charisma, psychology degree, a knack for knowing the Xs and Os of football and a feel for the game served him well as a coach. So, too, did his astute judge of character and talent and willingness to delegate.

Everything he knew to be true about winning football games made him a big fan of a young man from Wheaton. His name was Chuck Long and Hayden recruited him in 1980 to come play at Iowa.

Despite lacking much of a throwing resume (Chuck's high school, Wheaton North, favored the run), the blonde-haired, young man relished hard work and showing up in the film and weight rooms and on the practice field to get better at his craft.

Chuck Long and his brother Andy. The graduate of Wheaton North High School (Illinois) was recruited by just three Division I schools: Northern Illinois, Northwestern and Iowa. Despite being lightly recruited and playing for a high school team that featured the run, Chuck went on to set every Iowa Hawkeyes' passing record, finished second to Bo Jackson for the 1985 Heisman and was a 1986 first round selection in the NFL Draft – No. 12 to the Detroit Lions.

At no time was this more evident than prior to the start of the 1982 season. Hayden had just recruited a bevy of new quarterbacks including strong-armed Pennsylvania native Mark Vlasic and Cornelius Robertson, a gifted athlete out of Compton Community College and California's top-ranked junior-college quarterback.

The news – and stepped up competition at quarterback – fueled Chuck's motivational fire. After sitting most of the 1981 season (his freshman year), he intended to be Iowa's starting quarterback and the only way he wouldn't be is if someone else outworked him.

And he wasn't about to let that happen.

In preparation for spring football practice in 1982, Chuck dedicated himself to sweating, learning and improving as a quarterback. While others may have taken of the downtown Iowa City nightlife, Chuck worked on throwing mechanics and spent extra time in the gym. He also immersed himself in studying tape to better understand defensive tendencies and Iowa's offensive schemes.

It wasn't a glamorous time for Chuck. There were no cameras around or people wanting interviews. No one asked for an autograph when he showed up at the weight room. No one was talking about Heisman trophies as he watched yet another reel of film or studied the playbook or the habits of the opposing teams' defensive backs.

By showing up when no one was looking, Chuck was preparing to outperform the competition on game day.

And he did. When he threw his last pass for Iowa in the 1986 Rose Bowl, Chuck had taken a snap in five bowl games, held every Iowa passing record, finished runner-up to Bo Jackson in the 1985 Heisman voting and was selected the 12th overall pick in the 1986 NFL Draft.

It's easy to shrink in the face of adversity and uncertainty. Or to bail when there's work to do or to jog instead of run when you think no one is looking.

But those hungry for success don't. They put forth the time and effort so they can rise to the occasion. They embrace the moment – big or small because they are prepared.

Leaders show up when others don't.

"A professor once told me that it's better to have tried and failed than succeeded at doing nothing," says Terry Rich, international speaker and author and retired Iowa Lottery president and CEO. "Even people who went to the moon were off course 90 percent of the time."

Rich, who is charismatic, a visionary and savvy marketer who served as CEO of the Blank Park Zoo (Des Moines), says when people fail the first time, most quit. Leaders don't.

Terry Rich served as CEO of the Blank Park Zoo in Des Moines (2003-09) before being named CEO of the Iowa Lottery Authority by Gov. Terry Branstad.

"They keep adjusting, just like the astronauts, and are always moving," he reassures. "Heck, I screwed up all the time. I had a lot of projects that failed. But I had successes because of those failures. *Try nothing and you're guaranteed to succeed at nothing. But show up and good things will eventually happen. Leaders know this. That's why they never stop trying.*"

•

"There's no shortcut to greatness."

Terry Branstad, U.S. Ambassador to China and Iowa's youngest and longest-serving governor

•

"Courage isn't about not being scared. It's doing it any way. Your knees may be shaking and your heart may be pounding, but courage is not about the absence of fear, it's about doing it any way."

JIM KNUTH, SR. VICE PRESIDENT, FARM CREDIT SERVICES OF AMERICA

•

When the Children's Therapy Center of the Quad Cities needed a spark to generate more income from its annual auction, Chuck Long showed up.

"His involvement has made all the difference," says Angie Peterson, the center's president and chief executive officer. "We've been friends for many years. He's one of the kindest people I know. Big heart. Loyal to the 'nth degree."

Chuck's involvement, which began in 1996, was the result of good fortune.

Peterson, an acquaintance of the former Iowa quarterback and his wife Lisa and fellow University of Iowa graduate, literally bumped into the pair while making a stop at a Brueggers Bagel shop in Cedar Rapids. She made the ask on the spot and Chuck agreed to meet and visit more. The rest is history.

"He was such a favorite of my parents from the time we met as sophomores at the University of Iowa," says Peterson. "(Hawkeyes teammate) Billy Happel, who I grew up with in Cedar Rapids, introduced us. Everybody I was associated with got to know Chuck. He is such a class act. Warm, kind hearted, loyal and a very funny person.

"You meet people throughout your life. You make friends in kindergarten and then in high school and then you go to college. That's a lot of people over a lifetime. I'm fortunate to have him as a wonderful friend in my life.

"Sure, you can lose touch as friends graduate and you have families and careers take you in different places. So it was simply amazing when Chuck and Lisa moved back to Cedar Rapids and the chance meeting at Brueggers. So many years had gone by, but the friendship was still there and he was willing to go out on a limb for me and for the Children's

Therapy Center. He knew Easter Seals and the good work we did as an organization. But he didn't know the leaders at that time in our organization, yet he volunteered to put his name on an event; he took a risk to be associated with an organization that he didn't know its day-to-day operations."

The timing was right. Chuck wanted to be part of something – he knew his name could be used for the betterment of so many children.

"It touched my heart that he had that faith in me," says Peterson. "His name and face opens a lot of doors. We would not be the successful organization we are and would not be here after almost 70 years if it wasn't for him coming on board in 1996 and lending his name to this effort, being part of this organization and joining our board in 2013.

"He comes to our events. He participates like everyone else. When he goes around and does speaking engagements, he always talks about our organization and shares our story and mission. I can't thank him enough for giving so much of himself to help hundreds of children each year. He's pretty special but it doesn't surprise me because that's just who he is.

"Leaders show up when called."

•

"I want my players and children to know that nothing comes easy. You don't deserve anything. You earn everything. You must take responsibility for the things you do. That's the first thing I teach my players, my children and myself. I'm responsible for my actions, positive or negative."

JONATHAN HAYES, IOWA HAWKEYES' TIGHT END (1981-'84);
FORMER TIGHT ENDS COACH, CINCINNATI BENGALS

•

IT STARTS WITH ME

"I never wanted to let anyone down," says John Campbell, respected and beloved sports director for KCRG-TV (Cedar Rapids). "If I was sent somewhere on assignment, I wanted to make sure I got the stories and did them well and had them back here on time. Showing up on time and doing good work has always meant a lot to me."

Preparation meant arriving to work ready to do the job and do it well, he says. That meant showing up early to assignments so he could get his bearings straight and not rush what needed to get done.

"Looking back, I was always shocked when a game would kick at 1 p.m. and I'd see a reporter arrive at 12:57. I'm an 'arrive-three-hours-before-kickoff' person so I can check out the logistics and where the locker rooms are and make sure my cameras are working and stuff like that. But others just weren't willing to do that. They were willing to leave too much to chance."

"These are little things, I know," John added. "But be attentive to the little things and show up ready to work when you're on the clock."

John also took tremendous satisfaction out of meeting deadlines, hitting a home run when telling a story and making an impact by capturing the sights and sounds in a compelling way.

Iowa Football Coach Hayden Fry (left) and John Campbell.

"Of course, your viewers will let you know if you don't," he says with a chuckle. "For example, I'd work my tail off on a story and ask my wife later that night what she thought about the story. She'd simply reply, 'it was OK,' and then be on her way. Then I'd go in the next day and bat something out in 20 minutes because that's all the time I had; and I'd go home and she'd volunteer, 'Now John, that was a great story!'

"Being successful means showing up every day and giving your best effort, without fail."

CARRY YOUR OWN PAIL

Hap Peterson saw real-life examples of mental and physical toughness—how to overcome adversity and pain and persevere as an Iowa Hawkeye football player. It was how the team rolled under coach Hayden Fry. Every member of the team had to live up to expectations and uphold the honor of not letting your teammates down, he says.

"You had to carry your own pail of water because no one was going to lift it for you," says Hap while recalling the toughness, actions and character of fellow Hawkeye teammates and linemen Pat Dean, Mark Bortz, Todd Simonsen, Andre Tippet, Joey Levelis, and Bruce Kittle, to name just a few.

"These were guys I could relate to," he says. "You look at someone like Bruce Kittle; he blew his ACL out his senior season but there was no way he *wasn't* going to play in the Rose Bowl. So he gutted out the Rose Bowl while playing without an ACL. That kind of physical and mental toughness and what it meant to be there for your teammates—your brothers—was enough to make others want to overcome serious injuries and setbacks and play even harder."

Then there was teammate Bob Stoops, who, halfway through his senior season as a Hawkeye, broke his foot and had it in a cast literally from Sunday to Friday each week.

"But when Friday arrived, they'd cut off the cast and he'd hobble through walk-throughs before playing Saturday full-out on a broken foot," Peterson says. "Coaches like Barry Alvarez and Dan McCarney literally drove it in our heads that you cannot let your teammates down. You better show up and you better hold up your end of the bargain. And every player did."

WILL YOU FOLD OR STAND TALL?

"How we face adversity defines who we are in everything we do because there will be times you get the wind knocked out of you," says John Quinn, Waukee, Iowa, Chief of Police. "Will you crumble and fold or stand up and be the man or woman that you can be? Look closely at every situation, the way you react, the example you set and how you go about finding success through adversity.

"I tell young people, 'Don't find a permanent solution to a temporary problem.' Keep a long-term perspective rather than living for the moment and reacting to the moment. Be a positive role model by keeping life and what happens during life in perspective."

ONE OF NEARLY 100

"I've always grabbed my lunch pail to come to work and operated with supreme self-confidence in my ability," says Cascade, Iowa-native and sports broadcaster Gary Dolphin.

"To be successful, you have to show up knowing you can do the job. Don't change who you are because over time, people will grow to like your style. Even if they don't like it, they'll certainly grow to accept it."

Gary knows from experience having stepped in for legendary broadcaster Jim Zabel as the voice of the Hawkeyes in 1996. The transition also provided Gary with another pearl of wisdom:

"Don't ever think your style will endear you to every customer or teammate," he says. "You're never going to satisfy 100 percent of the people 100 percent of the time."

But just as important is the respect you'll earn by being authentic and putting in the time and effort and showing up every day ready to do your best.

"They may not accept your style, but they'll respect you and put up with you as long as you deliver a good product," says Gary, who was one of nearly 100 applicants for the Iowa Hawkeyes' broadcasting gig. "If you are good at what you do, they'll grow to like you.

"And for the most part, that's happened during my career," he says. "Now, I have no doubt that there are still people out there today who are upset that I took to the Hawkeye press box in place of the legendary Zabel.

"But if you do the math, we're more than 20 years into this deal. I've gotten a couple of generations now…one that's 19 years old and another that's 8, 9, 10 and they're listening and going to Hawkeye football and basketball games. They have no clue who Jim Zabel and Ron Gonder and Bob Brooks are.

"I guess you could say that's how the cycle works. It will be the same way for me when I disappear and the person who replaces me takes the reins and creates their legacy.

"They'll be successful too if they come in with their lunch bucket in hand and stay true to who they are."

They'll be successful if they continually *show up*.

•

That's what Jonathan Hayes, long-time assistant coach for the Cincinnati Bengals, loves about football.

"You better put in the time and have close bonds with the people you work with. Because if you don't, you won't make it as an individual because it will show in your performance.

"You quickly find out in this game the guys who aren't mentally tough enough. Leaders are strong. They understand what makes them tick and how to make others around them better. Leaders aren't flashy. They are solid because they have substance and others rally to that."

•

Leaders continually show up for their teams.

"Drive – have something to wake up to and go do it. That's what successful people do," says Terry Rich, author of *Dare to Dream, Dare to Act* and former Chief Executive Officer of the Des Moines Blank Park Zoo. "They get up and get at it. Even though they could retire, they're still doing business. They like being part of the deal and deriving self-worth from showing up and making things happen.

"They get excited by doing."

REFLECTIONS

Do you show up on time for meetings and appointments? If not, how can you start?

_____

_____

_____

_____

Do you remember and acknowledge meaningful birthdays and anniversaries? If not, begin by recognizing two people this month.

_____

_____

_____

_____

Join a civic organization. If you're already a member, volunteer to serve on a committee.

_____

_____

_____

_____

Work Hard (even when you don't have to)

There's no shortcut to success. It takes effort. What often separates those who achieve from those who don't is work ethic.

Rolling up your sleeves and digging in isn't as popular as it once was. The "easy button" seems to often be the preferred option for most people. Staying up late or getting up early isn't cool. In fact, it seems popular to find ways to work less. Expecting others to work hard is also, it seems, falling out of fashion.

Raised in Atlantic, Iowa, Kirk Tyler learned the importance of hard work from the get-go. By the time he was a senior in high school, the lanky young man had performed every job in the family-owned Coca-Cola bottling company, including sweeping floors and sorting bottles.

"I did all the jobs others didn't want to do," he recalled. "Without even knowing it, I was ready for the opportunity that arrived when I least expected."

Getting after it comes with the territory when there's a company to run. And that especially holds true when its roots are planted deep in the southwest Iowa communities of Atlantic and Villisca and it's been in the family for generations.

In fact, Atlantic Bottling Company is itself an inspiring Iowa success story!

Founded around 1909 by Frank P. "Perk" Tyler, the company built a reputation selling ice cream and soda nicknamed "Tyler's Flavors." Sales were so strong that Frank's sons Royal, Harry and Henry acquired a creamery in Clarinda, Iowa.

Upon opening the creamery, they discovered a franchise contract for Coca-Cola nestled in the company safe. The Tylers had heard of this product and its success elsewhere, but Iowans weren't familiar with it. So, they did what any entrepreneur would do: they embarked on producing and selling the Coca-Cola product.

Kirk Tyler, senior portrait, Atlantic High School Trojans (1974).

As with most new products, sales started slow. To help jump-start interest, they added a few bottles of Coca-Cola to the cases of Tyler's Flavors. In no time, Iowans were requesting more Coke.

In 1923, Royal sold his interest to Harry and Henry, who continued expanding the business by purchasing four additional bottling companies in Shenandoah, Atlantic, and Creston, Iowa and Grand Island, Nebraska.

By 1930, the Tyler Brothers had sold their ice cream business so they could concentrate fully on soft drinks. In 1949, Harry and Henry divided their business by drawing straws. Harry got Atlantic and Creston; Henry got Shenandoah and Grand Island.

When 1958 arrived, Harry's son, Jim, was managing the company, serving customers in a 60-mile radius of Atlantic with Coca-Cola and Tyler's Flavors products. The company had 16 employees. Just ten years later, the company expanded to 40 employees and increased its offerings to include Squirt, Dr. Pepper, Frostie, Root Beer, 7-Up and Tab.

On April 1, 1975, Atlantic Coca-Cola Bottling purchased the Des Moines area Coca-Cola franchise, and quickly burgeoned the brand's presence and popularity. This was accomplished in large part by Jim's son, Kirk, who was placed in charge of sales for the company in 1981.

Today, Atlantic Bottling Company remains a privately-owned, independent bottler and distributor of Coca-Cola products doing business in Iowa, Illinois, Wisconsin, Minnesota and Missouri. The company operates from nine Iowa locations with its headquarters still located in Atlantic, Iowa.

"Few could have imagined the growth but we've worked hard and tried to keep things simple," says Kirk, adding that once upon a time, the size of Coca-Cola territories was determined by how far you could go out from the warehouse or bottling plant by horse and buggy and make it back the same day.

Making decisions also matters. Decisions are powerful. They can shape the future in ways not imagined. Not making a decision is also a decision. But that doesn't apply to Kirk.

"I remember being a senior year in high school and my dad coming home one evening and saying, 'Let's go out to the country club and have dinner.' And that's when he explained the opportunity he and my grandfather had to buy the Des Moines Coca-Cola franchise. Oddly enough, it was, at the time, one of the two worst Coke markets in the country."

After explaining the opportunity, Jim told Kirk that he was not going to work to build the franchise in another territory unless his son was interested in taking on additional responsibilities in the business.

"So there I was my senior year. Heck, I didn't even know if I wanted to go to prom that year let alone manage a business. But he posed the question and I committed myself that night by saying I was interested."

Kirk soon enrolled in college in Blair, Nebraska, and then moved to Creston where he helped in the warehouse and managed a route for two years. In 1980, he enrolled in Coca-Cola's "S.O.B. Program" ("Son of a Bottler") and was energized by the experience.

"I really took to the business as a result and traveled the country, participating in numerous training programs. I also met a lot of great people. Putting in the time and networking are incredibly important. There are people I know today who I first met at that program.

"Regardless of the work you do, never underestimate the importance of meeting people and establishing relationships. Devoting time to making connections will positively impact you and your success for years."

•

Hayden Fry, who I (the author) had the opportunity to interview December 2015 for Chuck Long's biography *Destined for Greatness*, also embraced hard work.

"I remember getting my first paycheck when I arrived at Southern Methodist University as head coach," he said. "I looked at it and said, 'My gosh, that's not as much as I was making as an assistant coach at Arkansas.'

"But my daddy, who was a farmer, taught me these words of wisdom: 'Son, if you do a really good job and work hard and apply yourself, they'll take care of you. If you do a bad job, they'll fire you.' So that was my philosophy. And during all my career, I really never read a contract because I remembered my dad's words of wisdom."

Chuck Long, who was a "take-a-chance kid" recruited by Hayden in 1980, relished working hard to be a Big Ten quarterback.

"Many things – good or bad – can be habit forming if you do them enough. Hard work is no different," Chuck says. "Soon, working hard at something became a habit. Not being afraid to outwork the competition kept me sharp. And it kept me in the game."

Do you look for opportunities to do more? Stay the extra hour? Make the extra call? Knock on one more door? Put in the time and effort when it's not required? If you do, you'll quickly stand out in a crowd and separate yourself from the pack.

•

"I had a summer job my senior year at Iowa. We built a house for a farmer out on his property near Iowa City. We carried cement. It was hard, backbreaking work. But you came to appreciate what work ethic was all about. You got there when the sun came up and you went until 4 p.m. when you had to get back to campus and do some strength training. Hard work molds you and helps you do great things."

JONATHAN HAYES, IOWA HAWKEYE TIGHT END (1981-'84)
AND FORMER CINCINNATI BENGALS ASSISTANT COACH

•

"There are two four-letter words that will never get you into trouble," says Terry Branstad, U.S. Ambassador to China and former Governor of Iowa.

"Hard work."

And that is true for every successful business person. But hard work isn't delegated only to the world of business. Parents play an important role in modeling work ethic for their children.

"My parents, and especially my father, instilled in me the importance of always working hard and giving my best," says Angie Peterson, president and chief executive officer of the Children's Therapy Center of the Quad Cities. "They were both born in Monticello, Iowa, and neither into families that were wealthy."

Her dad was the first in his family to graduate from college—the University of Iowa Dental College in 1963. Angie's mother was a Mount Mercy nursing graduate and got a job immediately out of college at the Veterans Administration Hospital in Iowa City. After getting married, the couple moved into a trailer park in Iowa City with a lot of other medical and dental students.

"Mom worked to put my dad through dental school and dad worked hard because he wanted his family to have a better life than he had growing up," Peterson says.

Angie Peterson with Stacey, a client of the Children's Therapy Center of the Quad Cities. Stacey, diagnosed with Moyamoya, has benefited from occupational therapy offered by the Center. "These kids work hard to overcome some very difficult physical challenges," says an enthusiastic Peterson. "So we make sure they have a lot of fun when they're here. Fun plus consistency equals outcomes!"

She recalls the two pieces of advice he always shared.

"The first was 'Remember where you came from' and the second, 'Always be grateful for the opportunity you have every single day because you just don't know what will happen from day to day. You just have to be grateful when you get up each morning that you have another day to help someone.'"

That advice motivated Peterson at an early age to pay it forward.

"When I started first grade, I got the envelopes for tithing at church. I'd iron my dad's white office jackets and his handkerchiefs as part of my weekly chores to earn an allowance. A portion of that money was given each Sunday at mass.

"My parents watched to make sure that some of that money was in the envelope. I learned at an early age to be grateful, work hard every day, and give back. Those are things we're all capable of doing."

•

Jim Knuth of Farm Credit Services of America vividly recalls lessons taught by his father and mother, Russ and Donna.

"They demonstrated the value of hard work. Often that's not a fun lesson to learn. There are a lot of clichés about work but I truly believe, eventually, 'You get what you earn.'"

In 1979, hard work paid off for Jim. In the final game in his first season as an Iowa State Cyclone, he became the university's first freshman receiver to surpass 100 yards receiving in a game. That was a shining moment for Knuth.

"Hard work pays off, perhaps not always as soon as you want," he says. "But when you put your shoulder to a goal or something you're striving for, you never have to look back and wonder, 'What if?' I had supportive parents who taught me the value of hard work and it has made all the difference."

•

When it came to working hard sports broadcaster Gary Dolphin didn't have a choice.

The oldest of seven children, Gary's father died when he was just a high school freshman. His youngest brother was just two.

"Pretty much all of us seven kids—four boys and three girls—quickly understood that 'Hey, mom can't raise seven children by herself so we've got to get out there and help her out,'" he says.

"So we all dropped some sports activities to take on jobs to earn money and help pay our way. I was pumping gas by age 14 and worked throughout high school. I still played basketball and ran some track but understood where my priorities were and that all of us kids needed to pull in the same direction."

And that's when Gary learned that no one will give you anything—that you must work hard to earn your way.

"My parents and grandparents ran a combination grocery store and gas station in those early years, which, come to think of it, was probably a convenience store long before it was called a 'convenience store.' It had feed scales and ice cream and candy and cold meats and a bar. Obviously, we all worked in the store in the late 50s, early 60s.

"We sold it when dad died and mom went to work at the *Cascade Pioneer and Advertiser*, the local newspaper," Gary recalls. "I helped out as best I could, pouring the molten metal into the molds, which ultimately became the bars that would be formulated for the old printing press. I did chores Wednesdays and Saturdays and then worked at the gas station the rest of the week before and after school. I learned, 'OK, this isn't 9-5 or 8-4; if you want to get ahead, you're going to have to put in the extra hours.'"

That's why to this day, 15-hour days don't bother Gary.

"Now, I'm in my mid-60s and physically, I can tell when the workload is catching up to me. So I try to pace myself and get to bed a bit earlier at night," Gary admits. "But growing up in small-town Iowa and facing adversity at an early age and learning the value of hard work at an early age has stuck with me and made me better in all walks of life."

•

"A positive attitude and strong work ethic. Those are the keys to leadership and achieving success. I tell kids and candidates for public service that the harder they work, the luckier they get. I never lost an election, largely because I outworked the other candidate. Hard work will take you a long ways."

TERRY BRANSTAD, U.S. AMBASSADOR TO CHINA

•

DETAILS, DETAILS, DETAILS

Even for a company as successful as Hy-Vee, success or failure happens one person, and one customer, and one event at a time.

"The execution at the store level all hinges around the 16-year-old," says Randy Edeker, the company's chairman, CEO and president. "Because the reality of our business is this: you can have the most glorious and grand plan on the entire planet, but if you can't articulate it and bring the 16-year-old and the people on the front lines who are going to implement it, then it's all lost.

"Our people who interact with the customer are the first point of contact. You have to pay attention to that detail. It's in the art of the communication and the explanation and it's bringing that cultural buy-in especially when the culture and company are 85-years-old and invested heavily in autonomy by empowering store managers to make decisions. Those are the details, and they come in a million different ways from how you hang a sign to the kinds of items you'll find in the bakery."

"Always remember that you truly never arrive, that you're really never a big deal," says Hy-Vee Chairman, CEO and President Randy Edeker. "When you understand this, you open yourself to having good things happen and making the most of your day and life."

To further make the point, Randy recounts a supermarket walkthrough with "Supermarket Guru" Phil Lempert. Upon invitation, Lempert toured one of Hy-Vee's Minneapolis, Minnesota stores. Randy wanted Lempert, known globally for his fresh take on food and identifying emerging consumer trends, to give a critical eye to Hy-Vee's approach to serving customers.

"I respect Phil because he'll hit you right between the eyes with what needs to be said; he doesn't hold anything back," Randy recalls.

And so Phil and Randy walked the entire store. Along the way, Phil reinforced the details of providing outstanding customer service and choice. It was, in Randy's words, a painful but extremely beneficial exercise. Overall, Phil was impressed by what he observed.

"After the tour, he looked at me and said, 'You're so on top of all the trends and the lifestyle evolution and everything that's happening in the food world. Now, all you need is a sign maker!'"

To reinforce his recommendation, Phil used Hy-Vee's approach to crafting spreads for its bagels.

"Phil turned to me during the tour and said, 'Randy, you take cream cheese direct from the refrigerator case, go to the produce aisle and get fresh blueberries and prepare fresh blueberry cream cheese every single morning in the bagel department.'

"But nowhere do you have a sign reading, 'blueberry cream cheese,' let alone one that proclaims, 'Blueberry cream cheese made fresh this morning by Helen using blueberries from our produce department.'

"Phil chided me, asking how many people make their blueberry cream cheese fresh each morning. They don't. They take it out of a tub and they scoop into another. Yet we do but don't take credit for it."

Those are the small details—the extra little minutes of hard work—that Randy says make all the difference in the world.

"We do these things all the time because it's our culture and how we believe business should be done. At times, we just take it for granted that everyone else does it so it's not an advantage or something that makes us better. Yet it does.

"So we're making more signs!"

LET'S GET AFTER IT

Bob Myers never said a word about how he would transform Ankeny-based Casey's General Store when he returned to Iowa after serving in the Army.

He didn't even ask what his starting salary would be. He just accepted an offer for employment and went to work.

Bob's work ethic was born from a modest, blue-collar upbringing and time spent in the U.S. Army. After attending jump school at Fort Benning, Georgia, he was assigned to the 101st Airborne Division in Fort Campbell. Following deployment to Vietnam in 1967, Bob served stints in Saudi Arabia and Germany before being assigned to the U.S. Embassy in Kuwait. He also served assignments in Ft. Hood, Texas, and Fort Leavenworth, Kansas.

But Bob soon found himself retired from the Army. He and his wife Janice began discussing where they wanted to put down roots. One option was Columbia, South Carolina, where they loved the weather and the people. Another was Springfield, Missouri. But both locations were far from central Iowa and family. With Bob's mother and

Bob Myers speaking to Casey's General Store employees at the opening of the company's second distribution center in Terre Haute, Indiana, February 2016. The other distribution center (the company's first) is in Ankeny, Iowa.

her siblings living in Des Moines, the couple decided to return to Iowa's capitol city.

Not one to sit still, Bob took a job with a Des Moines manufacturing facility. Not long after, he noticed that Casey's General Store, a food and fuel retailer with locations throughout the Midwest, was beginning construction of a new corporate headquarters.

"I sent an application to Don Lamberti and was hired because I had some engineering and management experience," Bob recalls. "I was brought on to be the facilities manager and also, through construction, to be one of two project managers representing Casey's. So that's how I got started. All that took place in 1988 and I went to work in January 1989.

"I was eager to get back to work and have purpose and meaning in my life," says Bob. "In fact, I was so eager I accepted the job without even asking what it payed. The money didn't matter. Having a purpose and being challenged did."

Work hard and let your actions do the talking.

•

In the book, *Iowa's Record Setting Governor*, by Mike Chapman, U.S. Ambassador to China and long-time Iowa Governor Terry Branstad highlights six ingredients for success. They are near and dear to his heart because he's lived them and, as a direct result, never lost an election.

"They define me because I believe in them," he says. "I've always liked to work, having grown up on a farm. Having a positive attitude also helps you enjoy what you do and get through the tough times."

The farm boy from Leland, Iowa, shared the following six ingredients for success as included in *Iowa's Record Setting Governor*:

1. **Positive attitude:** People with a positive attitude are fun to be around. They are enthusiastic and look for new opportunities with every setback.

2. **Set ambitious goals:** Leaders are people with a clear vision of what they want to accomplish. They set goals to achieve their vision and measure progress. To be successful, leaders must have the confidence of the people they lead, and that can be obtained

by clearly communicating the goals, repeating them often, and demonstrating progress to achieve them.

3. **Hard work:** "I learned at an early age growing up on a farm to work hard. If any task is worth doing, it's worth doing well. Really successful people put in extraordinary amounts of time and effort to accomplish each assignment very well. This is true for athletes, entrepreneurs, musicians and elected officials."

4. **Look for opportunities:** There is a human tendency to become comfortable doing things the way they have always been done. The really successful people are always looking for a simpler, safer, faster, more effective way to do things. Leaders always try to surround themselves with idea people, problem solvers, and risk takers who are constantly looking for a better way to accomplish a task.

5. **Adjust to changing circumstances:** If at first you don't succeed, try and try again. Learn from your mistakes and make changes and adjustments so that your proposal becomes more attractive to those who have constructively criticized it. Remember, most great inventions succeed after many failures.

6. **Give back:** Be generous and give credit to all who help you. Successful people give generously of their personal resources to encourage and help others.

Do these leadership strategies sound familiar? Do you recognize a theme?

You are destined for greatness. These tools can help. Now get at it!

REFLECTIONS

Where are you failing to give 100 percent?

_____

_____

_____

_____

Why?

_____

_____

_____

_____

What three things can you do this week to get back on track? Be specific. Log the results here.

_____

_____

_____

_____

Set an Example

There are many ways to set an example. What you do can be negative, or it can lift spirits, serve a cause, and elevate a company as a valued and respected corporate citizen.

Helping others is the Atlantic Bottling Company way. Kirk Tyler, its CEO and Chairman, said everyone who wears Coca-Cola's iconic logo lives the Coca-Cola brand.

"It's about offering a quality product, continually improving the service we provide our customers and benefiting the communities we do business," he says.

It's a mission and purpose the company lives.

"We always ask ourselves, 'In the territories we wish to grow, can the Tyler family make a difference in them with the Coca-Cola business? When considering the growth in 2016 that would occur by adding eastern Iowan, we knew we could and so we did."

An example of living the brand was Atlantic Bottling's decision to collaborate with University of Iowa football.

As the kick of the 2017 season approached, Kirk and the team brainstormed ways to "be involved in something truly outstanding." At the top of the list was the "Touchdown for Kids" program.

Founded with the strong support and backing of Iowa Hawkeyes' head football coach Kirk Ferentz, it offers fans an opportunity to financially support the University of Iowa Stead Family Children's Hospital and the families it serves. Located adjacent Kinnick Stadium, the hospital receives pledges made by fans of $1 or more for every touchdown scored.

"So we asked, 'Wouldn't it be cool to bring more attention to the need that exists at the hospital and to those who are receiving care?'" Kirk recalls. "And that's when something truly special kicked off at Kinnick."

Founded in 2017 by followers of Hawkeye Heaven, the tradition of fans and players turning and recognizing patients, guests and staff of the Stead Family Children's Hospital is poignant and heartwarming… a welcomed distraction for those peering down… an escape from the trials and setbacks that life sometimes offers.

Krista Young of the small, western Iowa town of Anita, is largely credited (albeit reluctantly) for getting the ball rolling, suggesting it would be cool if the Kinnick faithful would recognize those watching from the skies above.

Iowa Hawkeyes' communications pros and fans began promoting and soon, one of the best college football experiences was born! Since its debut, television networks delay commercial breaks at the end of the first quarter of home Iowa football games to broadcast it live. Opposing players and coaches join in — proof that some of life's challenges are of far greater importance than winning a football game.

And it has brought untold attention to the hospital as major media outlets, including ESPN, publicize "The Wave" and its beneficiary in full-length features to national and international audiences. Chicago Cubs' Anthony Rizzo dubbed it "the best college tradition of all time." Disney Sports agreed, naming "The Wave" winner of its annual Spirit Award.

"It's an amazing and moving tradition and one that we couldn't be more humbled to help support," says Kirk. "The Touchdown for Kids program is the perfect way for Coca-Cola to be more involved in the communities we serve and to give back to the places where our employees live, work and play.

"As a family, we've always had a give-back mentality, not unlike most Iowans," Kirk adds. "That's just what we do – and will continue."

"There are a lot of people taking but not a whole lot of people giving. You get more out of life by giving more in life."

HAP PETERSON, IOWA HAWKEYE (1981-85),
CHUCK LONG TEAMMATE AND ROOMMATE

•

COMMITTEE OF ONE

Suku Radia, retired Chief Executive Officer of Bankers Trust, admits to being a fanatic about raising money. He's also very good at it.

Since 1990, the immigrant from Uganda has raised more than $50 million for the community. "And I can account for every dollar," he states emphatically.

He's also a fanatic when it comes to supporting his community. That's because his family was evicted from their home country with only the clothes on their backs.

"We lost everything," Suku recalls. "I was in college when that happened. So when we arrived in Iowa, I enrolled at Iowa State University and graduated in two-and-a-half years. When I did, I had $4.87 to my name. I was broke.

"So there I was, a man without a country and had lost everything. I really had to work hard to earn enough to finish college. And what I will never forget is the kindness that was extended to me by the faculty and fellow students in Ames at Iowa State. It was so touching that I said to myself, 'I think I'm going to spend the rest of my life giving back and setting an example for others.'"

Few opportunities provided a bigger stage to do just that than when Des Moines decided it would apply to host the prestigious Solheim Cup—a golf tournament pitting America's best female golfers versus Europe's (a format modeled after the PGA's Ryder Cup).

When you need a big project done, and the resources to make it happen, you call Suku. And to his credit, he usually answers, as he did when he was invited to head the committee tasked with bringing the Solheim Cup to Des Moines.

Suku Radia, Iowa State University, June 1973.

"I was asked to chair the committee. I asked, 'Who is on the committee?' They answered, 'You have to find those you want to serve on the committee.' So I decided not to ask anyone—that it would be a committee of one. That works really good because you can meet whenever you want and it's very easy to make a decision."

Soon after accepting the the role of committee of one, Suku traveled to Daytona Beach to meet with Solheim Cup officials. They were surprised to meet a guy who, in Suku's own words, "could barely speak the language" and who appeared as just a party of one.

"I'm sure they were asking themselves, 'Why should we give Des Moines the Solheim Cup? It's just this one guy and he doesn't even look like he belongs in Iowa.' Well, they didn't know my resolve and how I wanted Iowa to set the very best example and make the very best impression in the history of the Solheim Cup."

And that's just what happened. With Suku's leadership and the support of hundreds of donors and thousands of volunteers,

Des Moines hosted the 2017 Solheim Cup. It proved to be the most successful in the tournament's history. With sunny, blue skies overhead, the Solheim Cup, played at Des Moines Golf and Country Club in West Des Moines, set attendance records and became the most-watched women's golf event in the history of the Ladies Professional Golf Association (LPGA).

In addition to demanding it be the best-run event in LPGA's storied history, Suku had one other condition when he agreed to "lead" the host committee.

"Before I raised one dime, I said, 'One-half of the net proceeds that come to Des Moines Golf and Country Club must be given to charities benefiting women and children in central Iowa. And by the way, this is not negotiable. If you're not willing to do this, then find someone else.'"

No one argued, even when Suku asked for the commitment in writing.

"So when we submitted the response for the request for proposals to the LPGA, we put that right on the front page. They were blown away. They said they had never seen something like that. And I assured them that it would happen. And it did.

"It set an example for all future Solheim Cups and the good that can come from the tournament," Suku added.

"And it was a reminder that true leaders must also set an example. That includes having a fiduciary obligation to help those in need.

"It was such an emotional and rewarding experience. I've been given so much. If I live for another 20 years, I will continue giving back. I'm still not sure I will ever be able to pay back that amount of kindness, but I know damn well I'm going to try."

Now that's an example every aspiring leader should emulate.

•

"Great teams always have one thing in common: they have great players who set an example for their teammates. One of the things that people hold leaders accountable for is talent acquisition. So if you want to be a better coach—and have more success—then get better players. Being a successful leader always starts with people: recruiting, hiring, deploying and retaining them."

JIM KNUTH, SR. VICE PRESIDENT,
FARM CREDIT SERVICES OF AMERICA

•

HELP OTHERS GET THERE, TOO

Mentorship and being a mentor was key to the personal and professional development of Dr. Angela Walker Franklin.

Named president of Des Moines University in March 2011, Franklin credits mentors—Dr. Louis Sullivan in particular—for helping her pursue dreams and achieve goals.

"I had a lot of doubts about what was next for me and what I wanted to do in my career," she says. "I thought I was just going to be a psychologist, yet was evolving away from being a practitioner and clinician. That was a little bit perplexing for me because here I had spent my whole career working to be a psychologist yet was moving further and further away from it. So there was sort of a disconnect; I felt as though I was losing my sense of identity in some ways."

So Franklin sought the input from her mentors, picking their brains and asking why they decided to do what they do. She asked them how they attained those positions and why and when they chose to shift gears in their careers.

"I spent a lot of time asking a lot of questions. I really valued those conversations and those who gave me their time to poke and prod a little bit to say what-if and how they decided that and what they were thinking when they made that decision," Franklin says.

"*I gathered a lot of people around me because I was open to asking questions and open to their input and what they had to say. Sometimes that can be difficult—to make yourself vulnerable and admit that you don't have all the answers and that you can't do it all yourself. They in turn gave me their time.*"

Franklin says it's the time provided by mentors that made the difference for her.

"I was eager to soak it all in. I was very open to asking questions and they allowed me to do that. I have a lot of appreciation to those individuals."

One of them was Sullivan, former president of Morehouse School of Medicine and Secretary of Health and Human Services under George H. W. Bush. Sullivan "was there for me from the beginning," says Franklin. "He's the one who said I can do this—that I can become a university president."

It's the time, commitment, and energy that comes with allowing someone to be a little more vulnerable and to answer their questions that can help someone evolve and advance in their career, says Franklin.

"That's something I didn't have from women because there were very few who were college presidents and available to me at the time. Those I did know about were far away and being new to their roles it was difficult for them to find the time to give back.

"I always said that if I got there, I'd make myself available for the next generation of future college leaders and presidents, in particular women because they weren't here for me. So it's all about giving people time— sitting down and talking with someone and asking someone how I can help, what do you want to know, what questions do you have. I'm doing that for people now. When people call for time, make time because it's likely someone made time for you.

"When you get there, help others do so, too."

•

Hayden Fry never had a timetable for rebuilding programs. But he did know and recognize the value of setting an example.

"There are always a lot of variables. I did everything I could to change the minuses to pluses—the uniforms, the way the players conducted themselves in the classroom as well as on the field, having them say, 'Yes, sir,' 'No sir' and 'Thank you.' I wanted them to take pride in their academic responsibilities as well as their bodies.

"The key is starting with the individual. Collectively you get a team. Not many coaches do that. They get too caught up in dealing with the

X's and O's and 'Let's run off tackle and pass.' They forget they're dealing with human beings and sensitivities."

•

"Discipline. Organization. Sacrifice for the betterment of your friends. Doing the right thing at the right time for the right reason. These things permeated throughout my whole life. They matter."

JOHN QUINN, WAUKEE (IOWA) CHIEF OF POLICE AND FORMER IOWA STATE UNIVERSITY QUARTERBACK

•

"Leadership is about people. My goal was to shift the focus from management processes and procedures – not that we eliminate any of them because you need those things – to leadership and leadership development. Developing leaders is the most important thing we do at Casey's. In our business and in any business, it's always been about people – whether it's about shareholders, our customers, our employees – these are the things that are important in life."

BOB MYERS, CEO (RETIRED), CASEY'S GENERAL STORE

•

"I was always leading by example. When in doubt, always begin by setting a good example. This is how dad raised me. Walk softly but carry a big stick. I was voted captain because of what I did, not what I said. At that time, I wasn't very comfortable with public speaking. It wasn't my thing to get up and speak in front of the team. I eventually grew into that role but early on, I was more quiet. Let your actions do the talking. Focus. Do your job and prepare. I always approached it that I needed to prepare more than anyone on the team. Preparation was my answer to leadership. Being prepared is setting a good example."

JONATHAN HAYES, IOWA HAWKEYE TIGHT END (1981-'84)
AND FORMER CINCINNATI BENGALS ASSISTANT COACH

•

Scott Raecker, Executive Director of The Robert D. and Billie Ray Center at Drake University, is fascinated by character. Just mention the topic and be prepared for Scott, a former state legislator and Grinnell College grad with his BA in political science and religious studies to engage in a two-hour conversation...or more.

The Raecker family (1966) Father Jim, brother Steve, Scott and mother Thieleane.

"Character competencies are the things reflected in all of our actions," Scott says when asked to define character and how it impacts others. *"Character is about discerning right from wrong and doing the right thing for the right reason even when no one is looking. Character is made up of our actions."*

Scott knows what he's talking about. His life journey has been filled with a multitude of character-building episodes—from growing up in

Waterloo, Iowa and taking a banking job in Denver after obtaining his degree from Grinnell to going on a first date with a girl name Martha on January 10, 1990 and asking her to marry him just five months later. Character can manifest itself in many ways, Scott explains. Most often, it's demonstrated through our actions. Knowing I was raised on a farm near West Bend, Iowa, he makes his explanation personal.

"Having been raised on a grain and livestock farm, your dad may not have talked to you about what respect or hard work look like or how to dress respectfully when going to church," Scott says. "But he likely lived it: What does a hard days' work look like? How to treat others with respect; he just did it."

Scott's dad exhibited the same behavior.

"He was a perfectionist. And I still remember the day my dad came home after my brother and I stacked a cord of wood. We were so proud that we had stacked that cord of wood for him. And he pointed out that we had done it wrong—that it would fall and so we had to do it all over again. Now he did not come out while we were doing it and talk about responsibility and accountability and respect. He joined us and showed us. That articulated these values better than words."

A person of sound character models an example that others would do well to emulate.

"Character is about my action. What can I do to today to act in a capacity of trust and treat others with respect regardless of how they treat me? What can I do to act responsibly and accept the consequences of the choices I make? Am I prepared to accept the responsibility to choose my own attitude? What can I do to be fair in the decisions I make? What can I do today to demonstrate a caring heart? What can I do to act as a good citizen? Those are the six pillars of good character."

Scott encourages people to lead from where they are by continually assessing their strengths and ways to get better.

"Character fulfills purpose and your reason for being. It's about servant leadership—focusing on what I can demonstrate to serve others. What balance do I have between moral and performance character?"

Inherent to character is servant leadership.

"We have seen during human history leaders who have lacked character," Scott says. "And it led to disastrous results. You can't just say you're looking for someone with character. It has to be character with purpose. The purpose is very important. Some have led out of fear and punitive measures.

"Leadership and character are inextricably woven. You can definitely lead without demonstrating moral character competencies of leadership. But true leaders are those I look to as mentors—those I want to emulate. I grew up being taught that loyalty means something. I hope it remains that way."

•

"Nobody really thought we could win," says Hayden Fry when reminiscing about his arrival in Iowa City after accepting the Hawkeye head coaching position.

"So first I had to establish a positive environment. And that takes a tremendous amount of work. It's more than Xs and Os, although that's a big part of it. I'm talking about leadership, discipline. The way players dress. The way they come on and off the field.

"Coaching is 90 percent selling," he says. "I don't care if your team is in business or taking the court or football field. It's about trying to get those around you to believe you when you say, 'If you'll do it this way, we'll win.' It's kinda' like Bill Graham. He's trying to convert people. I always tried to convert people to become winners."

ATTITUDE IS EVERYTHING

"Is it more difficult to find leaders today? I don't think so," says Kirk Tyler, CEO and Chairman of Atlantic Bottling Company. "I get very frustrated when I hear people who bash this generation or the next generation—who say that these kids don't want to work or put in the time."

Kirk's perspective is born from personal experience, including membership on the Coca-Cola Scholars Foundation board of directors.

"The program receives nearly 130,000 applications annually for about 250 scholarships," he says. "We had a winner from Valley High School (Des

Moines) in 2016. I attended senior night at Valley to present the $20,000 scholarship. I was blown away when learning that evening that Valley High School had five students who earned a perfect score on the ACT! And that's in just one senior class. Not to mention they had six or seven kids who already had earned their associate arts degree from Des Moines Area Community College before they received their high school diploma.

"I tell people to quit bashing this generation because there are a heck of a lot of young people out there who are smarter and want to work harder than my generation ever thought of."

Knowing these achievers exist is one thing. Finding them is another.

"You're not going to advertise in the paper and have them come knocking down your door," Tyler says. "You've got to go out and look for them. And holy cow, are they out there. You give me a positive attitude and someone who wants to achieve and we'll train them how to sell Coca-Cola!"

•

"Great leadership can make all the difference," says Des Moines businessman Doug Reichardt. "The key in sports, business and with any team is to find great talent—talent that can often exceed your skills."

A sign of a true leader, says the former board chairman of the Iowa Sports Foundation, is someone who creates new leaders who can set the right example for others.

"On the other hand, if you don't have the courage to challenge great producers who are toxic to the system, then the system rots from the inside out. What great leaders do is change the mentality of a program. Hayden Fry, for example, taught people how to win again. You have to know how to win. At the moment of the storm, you have to have people who can make the right judgements and calls and plays when everything around you is falling apart. You have to be able to check down, whether it's on the playing field or the business field. That's the difference between going 0-11 or 11-0."

•

During Kirk Ferentz's first year on the job as head coach at the University of Iowa, the staff and players gathered for the annual spring softball game.

Iowa football's winningest Coach, Kirk Ferentz (right), greeting the man and Hawkeyes' second-winningest coach who hired him in 1981 – Hayden Fry – at Hayden's home in suburban Dallas-Ft. Worth (April 2018).

"It's a tradition for the team as it helps build camaraderie and chemistry," says former Iowa Hawkeye quarterback and current Big Ten Network analyst Chuck Long. "And of course, you have a bunch of guys out there and we're all enjoying a lot of food and drink and having a good time and telling stories and swinging for the fences.

"But I'll never forget after the game, Kirk was the first guy out there to clean up. He's got a garbage bag and he's stuffing it full of paper cups and plates. So here's the head coach who's also the first guy cleaning up.

"About the same time, I remember the late coach Norm Parker looking over at me asking, 'He's a different kind of guy, isn't he?'"

Kirk set an example that day of what team is all about and that no one is above pitching in and doing what's needed to get a job done, said Chuck.

"It's that attitude that makes Kirk so successful and respected by his staff and players and a characteristic of true leadership."

•

There are few ways to set a better example than by offering a helping hand those in need. Yet sometimes people shrink from giving because they don't know how or how much.

Angie Peterson, president and chief executive officer of the Children's Therapy Center of the Quad Cities, understands.

"I find it very interesting that people struggle with the idea of giving back or how to give back," she says with empathy. "A way to overcome that is to always remember that it takes so little to change a life."

Consider a five-dollar bill. For most, it's not a lot of money in the grand scheme of things. Maybe a latte on the way to work. Two gallons of fuel. A dinner tip.

"But $5 a month to a family that is dealing with a devastating illness or diagnosis is a really big thing," Peterson says. "Five dollars a month helps pay the electric bill or buy medication. Most people pay $5 a day driving through Starbucks, and is your life changed dramatically if you don't have that cup of coffee? It's about perspective.

"Too often, we get wrapped up in our daily lives and don't think about what a $5 donation or a half-hour of your time just once a month can really do for an organization like ours," she adds. "We're all human and wired to some degree knowing that it's good to give back. But people sometimes overestimate or overthink what they actually can give back or how much – I think they worry that what they give is not enough.

"Yet it's the small things that add up. For an organization like ours, $5 or 30 minutes or an hour of your time makes a big difference. If you start doing something small and you know it makes an impact, then that makes it easier to make a bigger impact as you move along and can lead to bigger things down the road."

Peterson credits her parents for modeling the impact a small gesture or donation can have.

"I was raised to understand it only takes a spark," she says. "That little spark can fuel a fire and make a big difference. You'd be surprised by just getting started and providing a spark and how it, in terms of time or a donation, can make a big difference.

"We all have the power to change a life every single day, whether it's a smile on our face or just saying 'good morning' to someone else. I always told my children to say hello with a smile because you just never know what kind of day that person is having and what they are going through.

"Or if someone is being bullied or ignored at school…you take those two minutes and say 'hi' and ask them to sit with you at lunch; or if there's a child not eating, you go back through the line and get something for them. It just takes a little thing to change someone's life."

John Quinn (right) and son Mike enjoying Iowa State University Cyclones game day at Jack Trice Stadium, Ames, Iowa.

•

"How we face adversity defines who we are in everything we do. You're going to get the wind knocked out of you. Will you crumble and fold or stand up and be the man or woman that you can be? Look closely at every situation, the way you react, the example you set and how you go about finding success through adversity. I tell young people, 'Don't find a permanent solution to a temporary problem.' Keep a long-term perspective rather than living for the moment and reacting to the moment. Be a positive role model by keeping life and what happens during life in perspective."

JOHN QUINN, WAUKEE (IOWA) CHIEF OF POLICE

REFLECTIONS

What characteristics does a positive role model possess?

_____

_____

_____

_____

_____

_____

Which ones can you emulate more often?

_____

_____

_____

_____

_____

_____

9 Authenticity Matters

What does it mean to be "authentic"?

In business, it means a company whose products or processes remain consistent and true to its mission and vision—even after 40 years. For the individual, to be authentic is to be true to who you are every second of every day, even when the forces around you would try to change you.

Leaders are authentic.

What made Chuck a formidable foe and such a likable personality was that he rarely changed from hour to hour, week to week and year to year. What you saw was what you got 12 months and 365 days each year. Chuck never got too low or too high.

And he never tried to be someone he wasn't. Chuck was a sturdy, strong-armed quarterback who relished the feel of the pocket but could slide with the pressure to buy another second before delivering the ball. His mechanics weren't perfect, but they matched his style perfectly.

When quarterbacks coach Bill Snyder attempted to tweak his throwing motion during a practice his junior season (passes were too wobbly, Snyder claims), Coach Hayden Fry didn't take long to stop his assistant in his tracks.

"Coach Snyder, leave the kid alone; don't say anything else to him," the old Marine instructed.

"He didn't turn his thumb down when he released the ball, over-strided and wound up too much," Bill replied tartly.

Hayden would have none of it.

"Coach Snyder, remember, the result is what's important," the head coach scolded. "He's completing every pass. Leave him alone."

Chuck Long, Iowa football's all-time passing leader *(photo courtesy of University of Iowa Athletic Communications).*

Soon, the blood vessels began rising in Bill's neck and face. But he didn't respond. It was however, the last time Hayden ever corrected Coach Snyder.

"It was also the last time he ever corrected Chuck Long," Hayden added with a wry smile.

Chuck was who he was. Sure, some of his passes had a wobble. But 782 of his passes as a Hawkeye were completed, covering 10,461 yards. When he graduated, Chuck held nearly every Iowa passing record and still to this day owns the best completion percentage of any college quarterback who has attempted more than 1,000 career passes.

Chuck was a hard-working, intelligent and measured quarterback who simply won football games.

"He fascinates everyone around him," Fry told Don Doxsie of the *Cedar Rapids Gazette* in a 1983 column published on Christmas Day. "He never gets excited, never gets his head down after a loss, never gets bigheaded. You just know from being around Long, whether it's on the football field or in a bull session, that here's a guy who can't miss. There are no flaws in his armor."

Long went from budding prodigy to king-sized flop to promising quarterback all in a three-week span when he first came to Iowa, Doxsie wrote. "That might at least cause a 19-year-old brief bouts of bewilderment, but Long remained calm. Deep down inside, he knew he was better than those first two games (of the 1982 season)."

Being true to yourself can be a challenge especially when everyone else seems to know what's best for you and who you should be.

But don't be fooled. Resist with every fiber of your soul becoming someone you're not. Or something you're not. Stick with who you are and what makes you tick. Stay true to yourself. Be real. Mean what you say. Be consistent.

When you are genuine and authentic, others will notice. They will respect you. They will want to be around you. Be someone that others want to be around. You are after all, one of a kind!

•

Scott Raecker, Executive Director of The Robert D. and Billie Ray Center at Drake University, says, "My grandparents were very much accepting of the fact that life is hard and it can be tough to make ends meet sometimes and bad things will happen.

"Today, we too often think everything is disposable, including experiences that may be tough or difficult. We have a way of turning away from adversity rather than staying in the game and working to make things better or to change your fortunes."

But, Raecker says, it's intuitive for humans to crave loyalty.

"Loyalty is a great example of something that can at times be in conflict with itself. You see this in politics. You run for office. You're affiliated with a party and a party platform. You represent a district and have an impact all over the state. But you represent the people in your district first and foremost.

Scott Raecker (left) enjoying a special moment with Gov. Robert Ray. The 38th Governor of Iowa served from January 16, 1969 to January 14, 1983.

"So when public policy bills come up and you have to vote for them, you're asked by party leadership to be loyal to your party. But I wanted to be loyal to my constituents. Am I loyal to my constituents or my party and what happens when there's a conflict, even within yourself?

"Loyalty challenges people. A good rule of thumb is to be loyal to your core."

•

Bob Myers, retired CEO of Casey's General Store, says leaders attract a lot of attention. For good reason.

"People are always looking at you; always watching, so you best set a good example. The higher you go in leadership, the more people are looking at you.

"You're always under the spotlight so you must conduct yourself with strong moral character; that's all there is to it. You do that, you demonstrate that through your actions, there's nothing more powerful than that. Obviously, you have to live a moral life, one that's filled with honesty and integrity. And, in our case, to model the "4-Ps" – Positive. Proud. Polite. Professional. You have to live your life by example."

"Consistency matters. Being yourself matters," advises Gary Dolphin.

"In my days covering the Bears, I crossed paths a lot with Coach (Mike) Ditka. He was bombastic and would openly question you—didn't matter if you were a reporter or a player. But over the years, the players and media came to respect him because they came to know his style and respect the fact that he was a winner and he knew how to coach."

Gary says every leader has his or her own style.

"But, as Coach (Kirk) Ferentz says, in the end, 'All that matters is wins and losses,'" he adds. "And Kirk knows. He's a Hayden disciple and adheres to a lot of the things that Hayden did, including his desire to delegate. Now his philosophies are a bit different than Hayden's approach...In his time at Iowa, Kirk has never gotten away from who he is and that the team's priority is to run the football...But inwardly, Kirk is a very good at handling personnel and people; he's not really into the philosophy of using overpriced words when he's talking to his players."

Gary, who has attended many of Ferentz's pre-game pep talks, says Ferentz is authentically himself, especially when it comes to talking to his players.

"It basically goes: 'We're going to outwork the other guys. If you're here for a 9-to-5 or 8-to-4 job, then you're probably in the wrong place. You'll be at the back of the bus. To ultimately get where we're wanting to go, we're going to outwork the other guy.' And that's an approach that's served Kirk and the Iowa program well these many years, especially considering the Hawkeyes have had just two coaches in more than 40 years."

DRIVEN

Angie Peterson is driven to serve. It's an authentic characteristic of the Cedar Rapids native who serves as president and chief executive officer of the Children's Therapy Center of the Quad Cities. The Center, which derives considerable funding from an annual charity auction headlined by Chuck Long, is a perfect fit for Peterson.

Her belief in what she does and who she serves didn't come from a book or watching TV. After a stint as public relations manager for an auto dealership in Phoenix, Arizona, following her graduation from Iowa, Peterson returned to the Hawkeye State to work on her MBA. Soon after, she accepted a field marketing manager with a gift and collectible company out of the Chicago area. It evolved into a lot of travel and prohibited her from completing her MBA. But it was a corporate sponsor of the National Easter Seal Society that was ultimately a life changer for Peterson.

The Easter Seal Society has affiliates throughout the United States. Because Peterson's territory was Iowa and Wisconsin, she worked with the Des Moines affiliate. Each spring, Easter Seals held a national 24-hour fundraising telethon that would break each hour to allow local affiliates to telecast twenty-minute segments.

"I'd attend the telethon each year and present our donation checks from our corporate fundraising program," recalls Peterson. "But soon after, the Des Moines affiliates' development director that I had become friends with moved to the Quad Cities. He was aware I lived in Cedar Rapids and thought I needed to get involved with the Quad Cities area Easter Seals Foundation. So he asked me if I would be willing to present our corporate checks in the Quad Cities market rather than in Des Moines."

Peterson jumped at the opportunity and, one year later, was participating in her first telethon in the Quad Cities.

"And there I am waiting in the green room to go on the air and present our donation," says Peterson. "Soon, I'm introduced myself to a young couple with an adorable, dark-haired baby girl with spina bifida. We were just kind of visiting and I asked them, 'As a corporate sponsor, I'd like to know a bit more about what you like about the Easter Seal Foundation and how the funds we donate affect people locally in the Quad Cities.'

"The mom starts telling me that when you're pregnant with your first child, you have all of these hopes and dreams and think about what this child will accomplish throughout its life and then the child is born, and you get an unexpected diagnosis and you don't know what to do or where to turn. Then she says, 'What the Easter Seal Foundation has done is give us hope.'

"And it was right at that point that it really hit me—that running a therapy center to serve people isn't just about raising money. Sure, your resources are important; Easter Seals provides programs and equipment and services. But above all else, we're giving families hope. We're giving children a chance to achieve the highest level of independence later on in life.

"There's not a calling in life as important or authentic as that."

•

A key to being a true leader is caring about people.

When Gene Meyer, president of the Greater Des Moines Partnership, was Iowa's commissioner of public safety, he'd visit with the custodial staff and ask how they were doing and the kind of day they were having.

Gene Meyer greets President George W. Bush at the Emergency Operations Center in Cedar Rapids, Iowa, to discuss the 2008 floods.

"That was just as important to me as seeing the colonel or the director of the department," he says. "*Helping people understand that they are making a contribution and that their individual contribution to the organization, no matter what it is, is vital to the overall success of the organization is critical.* That's the basic tenant. Once you do that, you're building a core team that understands and values what you're wanting to accomplish as an organization or institution. If you appreciate teamwork and respect it and foster it, just imagine how it will permeate throughout the organization."

•

Randy Edeker says Hy-Vee's goal isn't to be flashy. The same applies to being a leader.

"I may be strange this way, but I don't want the flash," he says. "I want to deliver real service in our stores and products that are fresh and taste good."

These goals are what led Hy-Vee to provide customers with a helping hand from dieticians. Prior to making that investment, the only dieticians in many of Iowa's less populated towns and counties were stationed at the nearest hospital.

"If you had a heart attack, you'd meet them," Randy says. "But dieticians want to work on the front side of food. I said a long time ago, if you save people a nickel on pork and beans, they'll love you for a day. If you save a loved one's life, they'll love you forever."

"Marketing campaigns aren't what I'm looking for," Randy adds. "More than that, we have to prove ourselves or our customers won't believe what we say. Be authentic. Be real."

•

University of Iowa President Bruce Harreld doesn't mind getting his hands dirty and tackling projects and challenges that most would avoid. It's who he is.

First, he lent a hand opening offices in Chicago and Munich in a stint at Boston Consulting Group. Then he was off to Kraft Foods where he served as senior vice president in charge of the frozen food unit.

Not one to sit still, Harreld taught at Northwestern University before taking the top post at Boston Market, a fast-casual restaurant famous for its rotisserie chicken. Then, it was off to IBM and his biggest challenge to date: taking the role of senior vice president for 13 years that included overseeing a major organization restructuring that helped the company remain viable.

In 2008, he returned to Harvard Business School as an adjunct professor. Then, on Sept. 3, 2015, he was named the University of Iowa's 21st president. And all this occurred before he celebrated his 65th birthday.

"I'm proof that, regardless of the industry, you can be coached and be successful," says Harreld. ***"Being able to perform is about people.***

Don't go to work for companies; go to work for individual people. I don't care what the brand or university. Wherever you go, make sure you know the people you're going to work for and make sure they have really good values."

Harreld admits he's been fortunate to travel the path he has.

"When you're going to be outside your element, you're going to make mistakes," he says. "You need coaches like I've had, who will take you aside and say, 'You may not know it, but you need a little help here.' Or at times when you know it to be true, then raise your hand and admit you're a little over your head and that you could using a helping hand.

"You need people around you those times who aren't going to fire you or take things out on you. You need a mentor, and I've had wonderful mentors."

Good mentors are authentic. Harreld says they understand their craft better than most. They never get comfortable with where they are and are willing to take the heat when things aren't going according to plan.

"You're either going up or down, you don't stay where you are as an institution, a company and individual. Leaders know that and keep doing things to experiment and try different things; they retool and rethink constantly."

Harreld says bad things will always happen, no matter the school, business, association or not-for-profit. There's no question about that. The more important question is how you react when they do.

"Do you paint over them? No way. Those situations are a teaching or coaching moment. You seize it and confront it and learn from it. You're always going to have up and down years. But do you have high values? That's what will carry you through any situation."

•

Few things are more authentic than character.

"Character is constantly shaped—and revealed," says Scott Raecker.

The former Iowa legislator, who now serves as executive director of The Robert D. and Billie Ray Center at Drake University, believes character must always be strengthened and sharpened "not because we are bad but because we can all become better."

When it comes to character, you don't need to be sick to get better; we can all become better, says Raecker, a native of Waterloo, Iowa who, in his own words, was raised in the "quintessential Norman Rockwellian Midwestern household.

"Our character is revealed in our choices and actions—our ability to discern right from wrong along with the courage, conviction, and commitment to do the right thing for the right reasons—regardless of the cost," he says.

Raecker believes character is revealed in our decisions and actions and developed through relationships. Character competencies are nurtured best with love and support of other individuals.

Scott Raecker alone in thought as he prepares comments for the 2017 ribbon cutting and opening of The Robert D. and Billie Ray Center at Drake University. "Character competencies are the things reflected in all of our actions," says Raecker, who serves as the center's executive director. "Character is about discerning right from wrong and doing the right thing for the right reason even when no one is looking. Character is made up of our actions." (A portrait of Robert D. and Billie Ray hangs the background).

"Character is developed first and foremost in the home through parents and caring family members," says Raecker. "Character is also shaped by any individual who comes into our lives in a meaningful relationship to help us become better—such as a teacher, coach, friend, or co-worker. To get better at character, we need self-discipline along with guidance and accountability from others."

Raecker, whose father was a dentist and mother an educator, says core values are at the heart of our character. So the ability to define and act upon our core values becomes important in shaping our character.

"For me, the Six Pillars of Character from CHARACTER COUNTS! are a simple way to distill the complexity of who I am as a person," he shares. "Core values should be thought of as 'I' and 'action.'"

For example, Scott says that to mold and improve character, he must ask, "What can I do today to act in a capacity worthy of trust?" And that's just for starters.

"Also ask what you can do to treat people with respect regardless of how they treat you, who they are, or what they think, and be responsible and accountable for the choices you make and the consequences of those choices," he says. "You must also demonstrate fairness by making decisions that are equitable to others, demonstrate a caring heart in your actions, and be a good citizen."

To be better at each of these, Scott recommends adopting a mindset of self-reflection of your own character and the accountability of at least one significant person in your life.

"You must also come to terms with our own character flaws," he adds. "None of us are perfect people, and I am certainly not. The only perfect person has already left this earth. We need to be held accountable for the choices we make, both good and bad, and grow and let go of our mistakes and missteps."

It's been said that character is revealed when no one's looking.

"Strengthening one's own character may best be characterized with a mindset that someone is always watching," says Scott.

"It's about continually sharpening the saw."

•

Jim Knuth, Sr. VP of Farm Credit Services of America, says success begins with surrounding yourself with quality people who want to be part of a team. Choosing the right people to be in the right place at the right time and doing the right things means being authentic when you hire them.

In his final game as a freshman for Iowa State (1979), Knuth caught 7 passes for 121 yards versus the Oklahoma State Cowboys. It was, at the time, the Cyclone record for most receiving yards in a game by a freshman. Only twice since has an ISU freshman receiver tallied more yards – Todd Blythe (2004) and Darius Darks (2008).

"It starts with people, not you," says Jim, who played wide receiver for Iowa State University before beginning a successful career in finance. "When it comes to identifying talented and engaged people, you know them when you see them—like the Golden State Warriors. When we look to hire people at Farm Credit, I sit down and tell people that I'm very clear on what we're looking for. I'm looking for people with:

- High values and high character. Our two core values are honesty and integrity. Period. That applies to everyone from CEO down. It's not negotiable.
- A passion for ag and rural America. It's all we do. It's a nice way to say that this is our purpose. You have to align with it.
- A desire to build relationships both internal and external. If you come here, you're part of a team. You have to be willing

to work in a team environment, and then, obviously, we build relationships with customers.

- A positive attitude and positive effort. These two traits are 90 percent of everything we do in life.

"If you have these four qualities, you can do great things here," he added. "We can teach everything else."

STRIVE TO BE THE FIRST CHOICE

Be humble and professional in all circumstances, encourages Dr. Angela Walker Franklin, president of Des Moines University. And that advice has served her well.

It was nearly a dozen years ago when Franklin, who was serving as Executive Vice President and Provost of Meharry Medical School in Nashville, was approached about interviewing for the position of president of an institution located in southern California.

Her long-time mentor, Dr. Louis Sullivan, had nominated Franklin for college presidencies. An active health policy leader and minority health advocate, Sullivan had served as the nation's 17th Secretary of the U.S. Department of Health and Human Services during President George H. W. Bush's Administration. He was also the Founding Dean of the Morehouse School of Medicine.

With Sullivan's encouragement and with each opportunity to interview, Franklin was becoming more competitive in the process, often finding herself as one of the final three candidates.

Now, after multiple rounds of interviews, Franklin was one of two candidates being considered for the California job.

"Dr. Sullivan, who was coaching me along the way, felt like I had this one," she recalls. "I had a wonderful visit on campus; the feedback from the campus community was very positive.

"And then I got to know who my competition was; it was the provost of Syracuse! So here she is, from a major university with a big name, and here I am, a provost from Meharry Medical College…a small and almost unknown entity on the east coast."

Dr. Angela Walker Franklin with mentor, Dr. Louis W. Sullivan, at Des Moines University commencement May 2016.

Franklin didn't like her chances, but she couldn't get an answer one way or the other.

"I had been on campus and I was among the final two…I knew that. But I also thought that surely, they would pick the candidate from the larger university and the instant credibility that comes with that name.

"Yet people from the campus who were hoping I would get the job began sharing that, 'Well, the campus really likes you but the board of trustees prefers the other big-name person.' I began to think which way would this go and how would it turn out. And time went on and on. But they wouldn't release me. They wouldn't tell me no and that they had chosen someone else."

Franklin admittedly became frustrated. So she turned to her mentor, Dr. Sullivan.

"I remember telling him this whole story," she says. "After hearing me out, his response was, 'Well, do you think they're holding you as a backup plan? That's what it sounds like to me. It seems the board likes the person from Syracuse and the board usually wins; they are the ones who hire the president even if the campus community likes you. So my guess is the board is going to offer her the job and if she says no, you're the backup plan.'"

After a pause, Sullivan added one more sage piece of advice.

"He told me, 'Angela, you should never have to play second fiddle to anyone. Withdraw from the search.' And I remember thinking to myself, 'Are you serious? Withdraw?' And he said again, 'You do not need to be the backup plan to anyone. If you are not the candidate everyone wants and is most valued and the best fit for the job, then it's clear you don't want that opportunity. Withdraw from the search. Trust me; there are better opportunities. You want to go to a place that wants you—that there's no doubt that it's the best fit and it's the right opportunity.'"

It was a tough recommendation. But later that same day, Franklin formally withdrew from the search.

"I just told them that the opportunity no longer felt like the right fit," she recalls. "They immediately called me and said they really hated to see me do that and asked if in fact I had made my final decision. I listened respectfully and just said I was sorry but I don't think this is right. And then I just waited to see what may come next."

Franklin didn't have to wait long. What she didn't know—perhaps it was divine intervention or fate—was that the same search firm that had brought forth the opportunity to go to southern California had also been hired by Des Moines University (DMU) to hire its next president following the departure of Terry Branstad.

Within a week of withdrawing from the search, she received a call asking if she would be interested in the DMU post.

"So here they were seeing me in this search; the consultant that was hired by the DMU was kind of watching and waiting because DMU was looking for someone with a health sciences background.

"And here I knew it was the same search firm and so I said, 'No, don't you understand, I've withdrawn from the search for the California university?' And they said, 'No, we are representing another university and we're interested in you.'

"It affirmed the good advice of Dr. Sullivan," Franklin says. "Here's an institution that's seriously interested in me and sees me as the right person for them. Yet I had no idea about Des Moines University or the city of Des Moines at the time, so I kept pushing the recruiter off, saying 'Well, I'm not sure I want to do a search right now.' Still they kept calling and asking.

"And here was Dr. Sullivan, again, my mentor, saying, 'Bingo! You have the institution that's pursuing you, that believes you're the right person for this job. You need to follow up and pursue this opportunity.'"

In March 2011, Franklin was named DMU's 15th president.

"So here I am, almost eight years later, still here and still having a great time. I'm having fun; there are real opportunities to continue to grow and transform this organization. It's a place I'm honored to serve."

REFLECTIONS

Where do you fall short personally and professionally?

_____

_____

_____

_____

How can you overcome these shortcomings?

_____

_____

_____

_____

How can you be more authentic to your co-workers? Family? Friends?

_____

_____

_____

_____

10

We Before Me

During an era of "me," when pop culture encourages attention on self, the team concept is becoming lost in the fog of self-absorption. Yet there's strength—and tremendous accomplishment—that comes through shared effort and sacrifice and putting team goals ahead of personal achievement and accolades.

Businesses that achieve goals often do so because employees are pulling the rope together in the same direction. Mountains can be moved when this happens.

"*Great teams are made up of great players*," says Jim Knuth, Sr. Vice President of Farm Credit Services of America.

Jim speaks from experience, thanks in large part to time spent on the football field.

As a wishbone quarterback for West Marshall High (State Center), Jim was tall and fast but didn't throw particularly well. When Iowa State University came calling, the plan was to redshirt the gifted athlete, add 20-40 pounds to his frame and transition him from offense to defense.

Given that the family farm Jim called home was just a short drive from Ames, the lanky lad arrived on campus immediately upon graduating from high school and got serious about working out and preparing for the physical rigors of Big 8 football.

"One day they asked me if I'd help catch passes for the quarterback and I readily agreed," Jim recalls. "Of course, I had never caught passes in

Jim Knuth's height and strength made him difficult to bring down as quarterback for West Marshall. When he did hit the turf, he was usually in the end zone, as was the case in this game versus Nevada, Iowa, his senior season (1978).

my life nor had I ever run a route. But that didn't stop me from lending a hand and helping out the quarterback and team any way I could.

"After a few weeks into summer drills, a coach came to me and asked if I'd like to try playing receiver," says Jim. "I said, 'Sure. I'll play anywhere.' So I started taking reps as receiver in the summer and that would be my position in the fall. I was going to be at the bottom of the depth chart and didn't realistically believe I would play."

But Jim was focused on being part of the team and doing whatever he could to help.

"I started to learn the position and when the season started, we had a couple of injuries. I went from sixth to fifth on the depth chart; then to fourth over several weeks. I kept working and learning how to be a receiver and eventually was placed in the starting rotation because I was open to what it took for our team to be successful and making the most of opportunity.

"I've never forgotten that lesson. It has served me well in all aspects of my life."

•

"This whole world is about relationships and teamwork. You build those relationships by getting engaged and involved and without having a specific agenda – just working for the common good."

GENE MEYER, PRESIDENT, GREATER DES MOINES PARTNERSHIP

•

"When looking for a job, identify companies that are a match for you, your interests and your passions. When you interview for a job, don't go in and talk about yourself. Think about the bigger picture. Put your goals in the context of what's important to the person who is interviewing you and the organization or company you want to work for. Ask how 'we' can be successful. Your expectations differing from what the company expects is how and where most people fail."

TERRY RICH, IOWA LOTTERY PRESIDENT AND CEO,
INTERNATIONAL SPEAKER, AUTHOR

•

"Hayden did away with the individual entrances onto the field, telling his players that running out of the tunnel, jumping up and down and high-fiving each other was 'an insecure type of energy.' Instead, he told them to trot onto the field 'strong and confident.' The 'swarm' was born and that tradition continues today."

AS REPORTED BY RANDY HARVEST OF THE LOS ANGELES TIMES
("FRY AID," OCT. 28, 1985)

•

A POSITIVE ATTITUDE IS A CHOICE

Being positive is a choice, says Kirk Tyler, CEO and Chairman of Atlantic Bottling Company.

"I don't want to arrive at the office in the morning, ask an employee how they're doing and hear, 'Oh, I'm OK.' Or, 'Not bad.' I want to be surrounded by positive people. So when someone asks me, I reply, 'I'm doing tremendous!'"

Complainers need not apply at Atlantic Bottling Company.

"I want people who bring answers," Kirk says. "People who exhibit being good and feeling good are the people who get things done. I like the people who feel great and are doing great today or say they're doing a lot better than the day before. It gives the day momentum and that leads to accomplishments."

A positive attitude also creates and builds relationships.

"I respect those who get out and talk to people who are in a similar situation or have similar challenges," Kirk says. "So be out and about. Meet people, get to know others and talk to people. They might not be able to help you right away, but they may know someone who can."

Tyler says too many people withdraw when faced with adversity. Leaders do the opposite.

"Get out and about and meet as many people as you can," he advises. "I encouraged my daughter to do that. I called her and she said, 'Dad, I'm at Christmas party hosted by Mark Cuban.' And I replied, 'Well, you listened.' Relationships and networking are so important. Get involved in service clubs. Write a book."

•

"I always try to instill in others the importance of always paying your civic rent. Become involved. You don't have to become over-involved, but start with one or two organizations. Show some promise and that you care about the well-being of others. It's important to give back."

SUKU RADIA, CHIEF EXECUTIVE OFFICER (RETIRED), BANKERS TRUST

"Sure! What do you need me to do?"

Angie Peterson, President and Chief Executive Officer of the Children's Therapy Center of the Quad Cities (CTCQC), got hooked on the organization the very moment she became a volunteer in the early 1990s.

Angie Peterson with College Football Hall of Famer and former Iowa Hawkeyes quarterback Chuck Long at the Children's Therapy Center of the Quad Cities' 21st charity auction (March 4, 2018). The auction, which bears Long's name, has raised nearly $1.5 million benefiting children like Liam (age 11).

When 1996 rolled around, Angie, a University of Iowa alum, was involved and ready to help take the CTCQC to the next level. More services were needed to serve more children. The center's celebrity sports auction was an important fundraiser but had been losing steam. It needed a name to bring greater interest and donations.

"I knew Chuck Long and his wife Lisa and their kids had just moved back to Cedar Rapids within the past year but we had lost touch after graduating as we had all gone our separate ways with life and careers.

"But here I was in Cedar Rapids, and I run into Chuck and Lisa at a Bruegger's Bagels one morning. After getting caught up on family and career since our Iowa days, I said, 'Chuck, this is such a coincidence but some of us at the Easter Seal Foundation in the Quad Cities were just talking about the sports auction idea again. Would you be up for a meeting to visit more about it?"

"And Chuck said, 'Sure.' Within a week, we met in Iowa City, pitched the idea to him and it didn't take long for Chuck to say, 'I'm in. What do you need me to do?'"

And that's how the Chuck Long Sports Auction – now the Chuck Long Charity Auction benefiting the Children's Therapy Center of the Quad Cities – came to be, says Angie with a smile.

"Knowing Chuck, I didn't think it would be a hard sell. What he always tells people is that he's from Illinois but Iowa was always his second home. So, it just really made sense that this event would be in the Quad Cities with an organization that serves children in both Illinois and Iowa. And, with his brother Andy having cerebral palsy and being an Easter Seals client for most of his life, it was just a no brainer because he knew the importance of the work that we did and he knows first-hand what consistent therapy did to help Andy improve his independence."

Nearly 22 years later, the CTCQC and its celebrity auction are going stronger than ever. The 2018 edition grossed nearly $150,000, a record. Since its founding, Chuck has helped raise more than $1.5 million.

"And it just keeps getting better," Angie says. "Chuck and I often visit that most events like this have a 5-10-year shelf life and here we are, going strong for 22 years. We're just amazed at how it continues to grow. Chuck and a passionate and dedicated group of volunteers have given so much to help others. It's amazing the good that can happen when people recognize the importance of serving others."

•

Those looking for purpose in life should consider two acts, recommends Scott Raecker, executive director of The Robert D. and Billie Ray Center.

The first is serving others: "Identify something that you can do to help someone else. Serving others in an area of interest to yourself will kindle the fire of passion that fuels purpose. To quote my mentor Governor Ray, *'The happiest people I know are the people doing things for other people.'*"

Second, Raecker encourages those seeking fulfillment to focus on the journey, not the destination.

"Purpose matters. The journey of purpose is built on two maxims from my mom: 'Remember who you are,' and, 'Enjoy the miracle of now.'"

Raecker says those aspiring for purpose in life must balance the inner peace of who they are and their life experiences with the passion for things they love to do in service to others.

"When you do those things, the miracle of now unfolds before our very eyes—in ourselves, our families, our friendships, our work, our community, and our world."

•

Visit with University of Iowa President Bruce Harreld and it won't take long until he is reciting the words of those who have had a profound impact on the human condition.

"I look at Mahatma Gandhi and his saying, 'There goes my people. I must follow them, for I am their leader.'"

Put another way, the best leaders are those who also follow. The concept may seem counterintuitive, yet it's worth pondering.

"Every now and then, ask yourself, 'How do I become a better follower?'" Harreld says. "True leaders are those who know who they are and always have a healthy, honest view of what they can and can't do."

That is why Harreld is a big believer in the value and role of teamwork.

"Many people form teams that are like themselves. I prefer to form teams that are totally diverse and totally unlike me because there are things I'm terrible at and somebody's got to do it. It's sort of like that offensive tackle on the left side; it's my blind side; you need 'em.

"Leaders know who they are. They also know who they aren't. They are thoughtful, values driven, and action oriented. They have a knack for knowing when to step up and take the reins and, just as important, when to let someone else."

This is especially true, Harreld adds, when things go awry.

"I have a really good friend who has a phrase that goes something like, *'Good leaders are good at the dance day-to-day; they know how to lead and when to follow.'*"

Rather than be on the dance floor, leaders will sometimes climb to the balcony and look down on the dance.

"At night, when leaders are alone and it's quiet, they're thinking about how the day went or the problem they're in. This, in essence, is looking down at things and observing them from afar," Harreld says.

"It's almost as if you're able to separate yourself and step outside of your body and ask, 'What am I doing wrong here or why is no one else understanding what I'm talking about?' Maybe it's because you didn't express the situation or the solution the right way."

So when things go bad, it's a moment of reckoning for leaders.

"That's when you must really listen, get feedback and not double down on the problem you've got and the way you're attacking it," he says.

Leaders learn a lot about themselves when they get into a situation in which things aren't going well. They know the right questions to ask. For example, did I analyze this wrong and maybe things aren't going well because I came up with the wrong idea? They observe and then come up with creative solutions.

•

"Leadership development and the enhancement of the human component of business is perhaps more important than anything else that we're doing. That requires positive leadership principles. My job as the Chief Executive Officer was to create the opportunity for others to succeed. That's my job. If I can do that, others will step forward and they'll make it happen. And they did."

BOB MYERS, CEO (RETIRED), CASEY'S GENERAL STORE

•

"Even if the ball is thrown high or low or wide, a good player always believes he's going to catch it. He wants to make the quarterback look good. This is the essence of teamwork. We're going to take accountability to save a play or make a play to make the others around us better."

JIM KNUTH, SR. VICE PRESIDENT, FARM CREDIT SERVICES OF AMERICA

•

Developing relationships to build a team for the purpose of accomplishing shared goals is very difficult.

Gene Meyer says those who think they can build and sustain relationships through the use of e-mail and all the different forms of social media are wrong.

"Every successful team is built around what's truly important to other team members, both in and out of the work or volunteer environment," he says. "It's a lot easier for me to disparage your ideas and not consider your thoughts and not care about your feelings if I don't know you.

Gene and Kathy Meyer with their granddaughter, Grace.

"But, if you're part of a team that has socialized together and gotten to know each other and understands what's important to each other, you'll give each other's thoughts and ideas much greater consideration. You'll also approach ideas others put forth much more professionally than you may otherwise, regardless of whether you think the idea has merit. So if you have a true team that is built on strong, interpersonal relationships, they'll treat each other with respect, regardless of whether they agree or disagree on individual topics or policies."

•

"There's no better example of what it means to be a team than the 2015 Iowa Hawkeyes' football team," says head coach Kirk Ferentz while recalling a squad that finished the regular season 12-0.

Kirk Ferentz

"What's ironic is that we were sitting as a staff in the office in April of that year. We're not quite halfway through spring practice and we're wondering what kind of team we're going to have and no clue as to what we could forecast for the team to accomplish.

"But again, that's the cool thing about sports," Ferentz adds. "It's like life; it's a dynamic process; things change day to day. And you're either getting better or worse."

For Kirk and his staff, the defining characteristic of the 2015 Hawkeyes who finished the regular season with an unblemished record was its great work ethic.

"The thing that really took off was the leadership base and that just continued to grow from spring through the summer and certainly throughout the fall. And with it, a real sense of accountability. It became a true team and it didn't matter whether you were first team or the 110th guy. Every player felt a commitment to each other and accountability to each other and they didn't want to let the next guy down," Ferentz says.

"These are things a coaching staff tries to teach and it was one of those years when everyone bought into the message. Leaders have a way of helping others buy in to a vision – a goal – and most importantly, what it takes to get there."

•

"I wasn't the greatest athlete. I didn't have the strongest arm. But I would get people into the right position and we would find a way to win. When you say team and all eyes are looking at you to advance forward and be successful, not too many people get to do that. But that experience is what we carry forward in life and it's pretty special to use the gifts given and the influencers in your life to do good and accomplish great things."

*JOHN QUINN, WAUKEE (IOWA) CHIEF OF POLICE AND
IOWA STATE UNIVERSITY QUARTERBACK*

•

There's so much to say about leadership, admits Scott Raecker. Perhaps it's because the definition of leadership is so broad.

"If you inspire people to do anything, you're leading," he says. "If you inspire a child to do homework, you're leading them. Leadership involves

the ability to identify and mobilize collective goals, mission, or vision; shared goals; the ability to motivate and persuade and empower others to achieve those goals; and the accountability of self and others around that.

"Shared goals. Motivate and empower. Accountability. If you're doing any of those things to inspire others, you're leading."

Not every day is going to be a good day, cautions Gary Dolphin, so be prepared.

The voice of the Iowa Hawkeyes recalls this important reality when broadcasting the 2016 Rose Bowl with Eddie Podolak, an Atlantic, Iowa native, and Iowa Hawkeye standout who played for more than a decade in the NFL for the Kansas City Chiefs.

"Early on in my career, a long-time and influential broadcaster told me, 'Gary, look, you're going to get your butt handed to you some day when you're on the air; your team is not always going to win; they'll get beat badly. There are days when you're just going to get blown out of the

On-farm candid of Jim Knuth, age 15 (1976).

water and you're going to get hammered on early and you better have a backup plan.'

"Put another way, you better have a sense of humor and chemistry with the folks you go to work with every day because some days, it's not going to go your way," Gary says.

·

How do you build a champion team or a company that's best in class? For Jim Knuth, the answer is not doing the same things over and over or staying in your comfort zone.

"We now have an unbelievably strong locker room," says the Sr. Vice President of Farm Credit Services of America, an Omaha-Nebraska based company that's consistently voted an Iowa Top Workplace by the Des Moines Register. "Our values, purpose and team work are the fabric of what we do. When you have a strong culture in the locker room, that's when you're at the point when you can do great things. Every championship team has a story about teamwork and chemistry.

"You really have to buy into the power of leadership, not management," Jim stresses. "I don't like to be anyone's boss or manager. I work with people. They don't work for me. Ultimately I'm accountable for many things and that's fine. But leadership isn't about title, power, or authority. And if that's what you're about, that's not a great long-term combination."

Jim says there's an easy test to determine whether you're a leader.

"Look behind you to see if anyone is following," he says. "If no one is, you're not a leader."

The Farm Credit Services of America team, says Jim, follows five basic leadership principles as outlined by Jim Kouzes and Barry Posner, co-authors of the award-winning, best-selling book, *The Leadership Challenge*:

1. **Inspire a shared vision.** Articulate a positive, uplifting future. Appeal to their values, their head, and their heart. People want to be engaged and play on a winning team.

2. **Enable others to act.** Everyone has the potential to be great. We don't put greatness into people. Rather, it's our responsibility to pull the greatness out. Assign accountability. Show visible

support. Then demonstrate it by asking a member of the team to lead a project and let them know that you trust their judgement.

3. **Encourage your heart.** Whether a kid or adult, we all respond better to some type of encouragement and positive feedback. Coaching from the negative only works for a short time."

4. **Model the way.** Jim says that when you're a leader "they watch you 24/7. Everything you do counts. It's about walking the walk. If you want true leadership, you model the way. If you don't walk the walk, you don't have true leadership. You may have authority and power, but if no one is following you, you're not a leader."

5. **Challenge the process.** "Move away from, 'That's the way we've always done it,'" advises Jim. "It's about strategy, choice, and proactive change. Stay ahead of the game by changing your company when nothing is broken."

REFLECTIONS

Identify two ways you can motivate a team with positivity. Do them this week.

_____

_____

_____

_____

_____

_____

Who do you know is ready to lead? How can you give them the opportunity?

_____

_____

_____

_____

_____

_____

11
Don't Rush It

Words to lead by. Advice to live by.

We live in a world that's always "on." Every lane is a fast lane. No one seems to have a moment to spare.

"Delayed gratification?" Never heard of it.

Christmas decorations, which went up before Halloween, come down Dec. 26.

Meaningful events are quickly forgotten as people eagerly look ahead to what's next.

The norm is arriving late and leaving early.

Why wait for the movie to come out in the theater when you can stream it live via Netflix now?

Savings? What's that?

Twelve-year-olds wish they could drive.

High school seniors have already completed enough course credits to qualify for a two-year college degree.

A team and coach, within moments of winning a championship, are asked about the prospects for a repeat.

Those who get elected one day are campaigning for reelection the next!

Patience is in short supply. With people in such a rush, conversations—at least the substantive ones—rarely happen.

Take your foot off the gas from time to time. Let life unfold and appreciate it. Take inventory of your blessings and accomplishments. And do so often. Relish the joys and the heartache. Pause and take a deep breath. Be silent. Exhale.

Then do it again.

•

"Often, greatness comes out of the blue. You don't know it's going to happen. There's nothing wrong with setting goals and striving to be something. But often, your greatness comes out of nowhere – when you least expect it. As a parent, I always support and encourage our children to do whatever they want to do. But don't rush it. Relax, do something you're good at and then work hard at. Be smart about what you do and always maintain a balance between rushing and striving."

LISA LONG, WIFE OF CHUCK LONG

•

When offering counsel to young people, retired Bankers Trust CEO Suku Radia pulls no punches.

"See that chip on your shoulder? Knock it off."

Sure, that young, aspiring leader may have a 4.0 grade point, but it is nothing more than a foundation.

"Rest assured," stresses Suku, who immigrated to the United States from Uganda in 1971, "this is nothing more than a good start. I remember when I was 16, I couldn't believe how stupid my father was. And soon, over the next five years, I couldn't believe how much smarter my father was. Never forget how much age and experience matter. Learn from those who are older and more experienced. Never be afraid to ask them questions.

"And please, please, please do not walk into a room thinking you have all the answers because you have a wonderful grade point. It's just a foundation, nothing more than that. You're going to need to develop

Suku Radia was raised in Uganda and moved to Iowa in 1971, enrolling at Iowa State University. From these humble beginnings, Radia earned national and international acclaim for his financial savvy and, even more important, his philanthrope and mentorship.

on that foundation. And that means being humble, you need to listen, you need to be a lifelong learner. And then you need to be prepared for whatever is asked of you and to deliver it and then some. It will show promise. It will show people you care. Others will notice and value you as a trusted member of a team who doesn't just have the smarts, but the character to go with it."

•

Take a breath.

"What's at the root of much of what challenges us today?" asks Waukee Police Chief John Quinn. "It's the breakdown of the family structure. It's the dual parents working in the world to make it. Too often, parents put the burden on TVs, games, kids, and others who aren't such a good influence. There are a lot of mental health issues. The heart and soul of what we face today is the single family house and a lack of the father structure in the family residence."

There's also a lack of patience in a culture that offers immediate access to all elements of evil.

"A disciplined home built on love and respect offers us the greatest opportunity to rediscover what can make our neighborhoods and communications strong again," John adds. "Not that long ago, you knew as a child what the line in the sand was and you didn't cross it, not because of the fear of retaliation but because you didn't want to disappoint. Now you have 'helicopter' parents; they hover over every aspect of the children but not always in a helpful way.

Children's schedules have also changed exponentially," John says. "Every minute of every day is focused on organized engagement. Gone are the days of sandlot baseball and football; fishing and making up games with children in the neighborhood. Unfortunately, you can't even let kids run free today and mingle with each other. No longer are they developing confidence and friendships and communication skills through positive social engagement. Today, cell phones and screens dominate the kids' mindset."

Young people also expect things at an earlier age. Quinn says they want things like a car and other material items so they get jobs to earn money rather than to be a kid and get involved in activities.

"We've lost patience and given up on parenting, with the burden now displaced to babysitters, day cares, schools, teachers, coaches, and law enforcement," he says. "It's unfortunate and changed things, and not for the better."

Don't rush things. Be patient. Be present. Make a positive difference. The world will be a better place because of it.

•

Bruce Rastetter, entrepreneur from Hubbard, Iowa, says, success takes time and patience.

"You have to work at being patient. No one can be an instant success, unless you just get lucky. But more often than not, success takes hard work and time."

Life comes at us at breakneck speed, adds Randy Edeker, Chairman, CEO and President of Hy-Vee Inc.

Store managers, he says, are always on the go. The obligations are constant. Decisions always need to be made. There are goals and expectations to exceed. Having to continually look ahead can make it difficult to be in the moment.

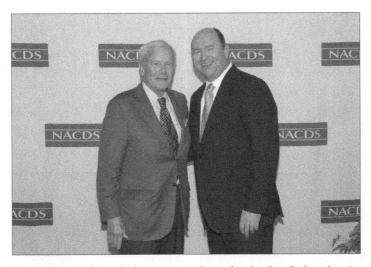

Randy Edeker (right) and television journalist and author Tom Brokaw. A native of Webster, South Dakota, Brokaw attended one year of studies at the University of Iowa. He's the only person to have hosted all three major NBC News programs including The Today Show, NBC Nightly News and Meet the Press.

But, urges Randy, do your best to stay grounded and make time for the present.

"Always remember that you truly never arrive—that you're really never a big deal; then you'd open yourself up to having good things happen and making the most of your day and life," he says.

When serving as the district supervisor for Hy-Vee in Kansas City, he awoke one day immediately knowing it was going to be a crazy, busy one. His schedule was packed. It was a day he was going to have to muscle through. One of his obligations was representing Hy-Vee at a recognition ceremony at the Negro Leagues Baseball Museum at the intersection of 18th and Vine in downtown Kansas City.

"I have so many other things to do," he says under his breathe.

Other tasks, he reasoned, were more important than attending a sponsorship recognition ceremony where Hy-Vee representatives and others were invited to be honored and participate in a private, guided tour.

"And I'm thinking, 'You know, they really don't need to do this; it's fine. We want to sponsor the museum but a tour really isn't necessary,'" Randy recalls.

But, out of respect for the league and Hy-Vee's reputation, Randy and others make their way downtown. Much to their surprise, legendary baseball player and coach Buck O'Neil shows up.

"He's nearly 90 years old, played for the Kansas City Monarchs, and he was the first black coach in Major League Baseball," Randy says. "I mean, it was absolutely a defining moment for me and my career. It's one of those occasions when you just stand there and are amazed by the stories he shared. It was completely unexpected.

"And it was the perfect reminder to slow down and never be too big for the moment because you think you've got too many things to do. *Keep in mind that others don't know who you are or how busy you are. They're sizing you up for the first time and forming an impression of what you're all about.*"

If you're always in a rush, you'll miss important and memorable moments, Randy adds.

Another time he learned this life lesson occurred when Randy was chairman of the National Association of Chain Drug Stores. Tom Brokaw was the keynote speaker for the organization's annual meeting.

"He's this larger than life guy. He's iconic," Randy says. "Everyone knows him and recognizes him. I recall walking into the green room to meet him. He's sitting in the chair and he's like, 'You're the Hy-Vee guy, right?' And I say, 'Yes, sir.' He replies, 'I need to personally thank you for single-handedly civilizing South Dakota.'"

Randy paused, then asked, "How did I do that, sir?"

Tom replies in his unmistakably baritone voice. "Because you brought Starbucks to Yankton."

They then proceed to visit for 45 minutes backstage.

"All the time, I'm reminding myself that I'm really a nobody in the grand scheme of things; I mean, I get it that I'm CEO of Hy-Vee and everything and we're a great company and we're a big company compared to some," Randy says. "But in the grand scheme of things, we're a small company. And here's Tom Brokaw—or Walter Cronkite two guys my age—taking that time to be interested and engaged. That meant a lot. It was an amazing opportunity, one I'll never forget, and an interaction that will always be inspirational for me."

REFLECTIONS

How can you slow down and be in the moment?

_____

_____

_____

_____

What three things should you worry less about?

_____

_____

_____

_____

List five blessings in your life. Make them visible so you can be reminded of them every day.

_____

_____

_____

_____

12 Enjoy Your Happy Place

Everyone thinks they know what's best for you. For every one signal caller, there are hundreds of armchair quarterbacks. They plan for you. Expect for you. Think for you.

"You've been in your job too long," they say. "You haven't been in your place of employment long enough," others say.

Or you live too far away from home. Or perhaps not far enough. Need to go back to school or been in school too long. If you're single, you should be married. If you're married, you should be single.

You're too thin. Not thin enough. Don't exercise enough. You're too active.

Ever notice how many people believe they know what's best for you? Ignore most of the arm chair quarterbacking. It's largely idle talk.

Meeting someone else's demands for being happy can be exhausting. Maybe it's best to enjoy life where you are—to be in the moment, not rush to the next place or the next thing.

As Hy-Vee's Randy Edeker says in the previous chapter, if you're always in a rush, you'll miss important and memorable moments.

Take time from doing and do some reflecting.

Do you want to be somewhere else? A different neighborhood? A different job? A different occupation?

Are you restless thinking you need to move on, be somewhere else, doing some different job because you think someone else wants you to?

Pause and think for a moment. Do you enjoy what you're doing? Is it fulfilling? Are you making a difference? Do you find the work challenging? Are the relationships fulfilling? Are you appreciated? Do you have opportunity to develop and grow personally and professionally?

If you can answer 'yes' to these questions, then enjoy where you are. Soak in what you have. Give thanks for the blessings you have.

So often, we think life is better somewhere else or doing something else, when in fact, we have the best of the best right where we are.

Being happy is about taking inventory of one's blessings.

•

Suku Radia, retired CEO of Bankers Trust and philanthropist, admits to learning much of what truly matters in life and as a leader from his children.

That includes being in the moment, like when you're at the dinner table.

"I've learned a lot from my children, starting with Natalie, my youngest," he says.

Suku and his wife Mary always read to their children. They were fanatics about reading to the children.

"So when we found out we were expecting, Mary was in Iowa City doing her fellowship. This is before cell phones. I called and said, 'Honey, put the phone to your tummy.' She replies, 'What?' And I said, 'I want to read to the baby.' Fifteen minutes later, Mary asks, 'Are you done?' And I said, 'No.' And she said, 'You know, these charges pile up.' And I said, 'We're not going broke.'

"This tradition continued and we read to every one of our children. One night, after finishing reading, our daughter Natalie said, 'Dad, I can do this one by myself. I don't need your help.' So, having learned never to argue with a woman, I decided I better leave the room.

"And as I'm walking out, I hear her begin the Lord's Prayer, which she knew the most...and she comes to the main part, the most important part, and I hear her sweet, little voice say, 'And deliver us from e-mail.' And I've always thought to myself, 'How true.'

"Very clearly, I have learned that it's easy to overdo it as a leader. I sometimes caught myself sitting at the dinner table with my phone. And soon Mary and I decided that we would no longer have our phones at the table, no matter what. It's important to have a conversation with your spouse and your family instead of looking at a phone or screen. Leaders make it a point to be in the moment, where you're needed the most."

The Radia family (1969), from left: Suku, mother Lila, father V.V. and brother Vibha.

Many coaches and youth leaders agree.

"We continually talk to players about the noise and distractions of life," says Iowa football coach Kirk Ferentz. "There are so many of them and social media is part of that.

"We tell our kids that the best part of life is the day to day and the people you get to interact with. That's the beauty of coaching. It's been a long time since I've played but one of the most enjoyable parts of the game is the teammates you take the field with and the experiences you have together.

"The same can be said for life. No matter what you do, you hope you find something that kind of grabs you a little bit and that you have a passion for and then it's just a matter of working at it daily. And along the way, enjoying the day to day and not just the game day stuff. It's not just the experience of playing the game but the stuff that goes with it. It's not just the job but the life that goes with it."

•

Most people seem to want to be somewhere else.

Not the long-time leader of Casey's General Store.

"I love Iowa," says Bob Myers, its retired CEO. "We're blessed to be born in Iowa and the Midwest where we have core values that stand out and are associated with this area of the country. We can be proud of our agricultural heritage and that it's really that agricultural heritage that is the keeper of our Midwestern values. Arguably, farmers are the ones that are displaying and conveying those sound values to us and have for so many year.

"So Casey's has a responsibility in our small, rural communities to do all the right things within them to embrace those Midwestern values and to share them and convey them to others. To take pride in where we're from.

"Our challenge at Casey's is to figure if we could build the kind of store that would make financial sense to place in a smaller, rural community and stabilize the population. We're working really hard on that small store design. We want to be an anchor for small communities and help them grow around that store."

•

"If I look back, I think about the amount of fun things I've been able to do. That's pretty cool. I've had a lot of crazy ideas and some of them have worked. That's what I'm most proud of. When I think of my biggest regret, it's that I haven't quite learned how to relax and to not stress out. It's a delicate balance not to work too much and to not coast too much."

TERRY RICH, IOWA LOTTERY PRESIDENT AND CEO (RETIRED),
INTERNATIONAL SPEAKER, AUTHOR

•

"Above all, you need to stay grounded," advises Angie Peterson, mother, volunteer and president and CEO of the Children's Therapy Center Quad Cities.

Easier said than done.

"I look back at when I graduated from college," Peterson says. "It was, 'Get done in four years, get a job and make money.' That was the mid-80s and there was too much excess of everything—too much make up, too much big hair; everything was big and living large."

Then, in the blink of an eye, you have to get a job, and get settled in your career; many people get married and start a family, Peterson adds. Very soon, you care even more about how you look and how you're perceived and what others think of you.

"You get a house, then a bigger house; then you need a bigger car and then the SUV and then the bigger house," Peterson says. "You're concerned about the appearance of success and wealth."

Angie Peterson with her children (from left) Michael, Phil and Abbie (Easter 2015).

But as you mature, she says, "You start going the other way; you realize that you don't need such a big house or all the stuff you've accumulated—that you need to simplify. That's when you realize there are things more important than the material things.

"I tell my kids, who are now in their 20s and 30s, that when they go to bed at night, at the end of the day, do you feel good about your day? Not every day is easy and everyone has challenges and there are days you say to yourself you can't do it or question what you're doing. But every day, can you think of one thing that you did that helped someone else or made someone else's day?

"And then, at the end of your life, when they're all there—and hopefully there's a big group to say goodbye—will they remember the car you drove, the house you lived in, the shoes you wore, the fabulous vacations you took, or how much money is in your bank account? Are those the things people will think about?

"Or if you could be a fly on the wall at your memorial service, wouldn't you rather have them say, 'Wow, she always made time for her kids or her friends,' or, 'He was always willing to help with something if you called him or always had a smile on his face or a good story to tell.'

"That's my advice," Peterson says. "Don't get caught up in the day to day and what you think you're supposed to have or how people judge you based on the things you have or the money you have. At the end of the day, did I do something good? Did I help someone in need? And at the end of your life, did I make a difference in someone else's' life?

"I believe everything happens for a reason and it can all work out in the end if you look out for other people. Just keep doing good things every day. That's what will create your legacy."

•

"You know, I've been battling cancer for a long time. And my doc has always said, 'Laughing and enjoying life are the best medicine.'"
COACH HAYDEN FRY, INTERVIEW WITH AARON PUTZE, DEC. 12, 2015

REFLECTIONS

How do you want to be remembered?

_____

_____

_____

_____

What do you want others to say about you when you are not around?

_____

_____

_____

_____

What can you start doing now to make that so?

_____

_____

_____

_____

13

Believe in Someone

Belief is having trust, faith and confidence in someone.

There are few motivators more powerful than this.

Believing in someone will make them stronger, happier, and more productive. In return, they'll believe in you, too, says Jim Knuth, Sr. Vice President of Farm Credit Services of America.

"In my office in Perry (Iowa), I have several wall hangings that are leadership focused," he says. "One of my favorites features the statement, 'I believe in you.'"

Those four words, whether in sports, business, or as a parent, are among the four most important you can say to a friend, a co-worker or a peer.

"That's because they can mean the difference between a fear of failure or the courage to try," Jim says. "It resonates with me because consciously or subconsciously, that's what my parents and high school football coach (Gary) Swenson and coach (Mack) Brown at Iowa State did for me and my journey.

"While they may not have said those four words, they communicated it through their actions and that changed me from a small-town boy having a fear of failure to having the courage to try."

Chuck Long was a quiet guy from Wheaton that wasn't heavily recruited while completing his senior year at Wheaton North High School located in the western suburbs of Chicago. In fact, only three schools expressed an interest: Iowa, Northern Illinois and Northwestern.

When called by Iowa assistant Bill Snyder and offered an opportunity to travel to Iowa City in December of 1980 for essentially a job interview, Chuck jumped at the chance.

After meeting the coaching staff, touring campus and enjoying prime rib at the Iowa River Power Company, Chuck wanted to be a Hawkeye on the spot.

Chuck Long and Iowa Hawkeyes' football coach Hayden Fry enjoying the moment at the 1985 Davey O'Brien Award ceremony. Chuck played in five bowl games and held every school passing record when he graduated in 1985. *(Photo University of Iowa Athletic Communications)*

"I remember Hayden calling me into his office on a Sunday after spending a couple of days on campus," Chuck says. "It was the last visit with the coach before returning to Wheaton. It was that conversation where the coach was going to say goodbye or offer a scholarship.

"And I remember walking into his office and sitting down on the big, leather couch. Hayden looked me square in the eye and said, 'Chuck, we're going to do some amazing things here. We're going to be successful. And I want you to be a part of it.

"It was his belief that he was going to turn things around at Iowa and a belief in me and my abilities and I could contribute that made me want to commit on the spot," Chuck says.

After returning home to Wheaton later that same day, it didn't take Chuck and his family long to take coach Fry up on his offer.

Looking back, Chuck was the perfect player for Hayden to bring on board at Iowa as he began building a winning program.

"The two got along so well because they listened to each other," says Gary Dolphin, the voice of the Iowa Hawkeyes. "Chuck listened to Hayden when he came calling on the recruiting trail and Chuck trusted Hayden that he meant it when he said he was going to bring a winning tradition to Iowa City."

But it wasn't all roses, Gary adds.

"Chuck would tell you off the record that there were a couple of times when he wanted to challenge Hayden and then Hayden would say, 'Chuck, run the damn play. It'll work. It'll work.'"

One of those moments was the naked bootleg Hayden called against Michigan State in 1985. Chuck faked the handoff to running back Ronnie Harmon and then scooted around into the end zone untouched, securing a 35-31 win against the pesky Spartans.

"That was one of those moments," says Gary. "Hayden told Chuck, 'I don't want you to tell anyone what you're doing. You just tell 'em that we're going to run the dive into the middle of the line with Harmon. But whatever you do, don't give the dang ball to Ronnie – you put it in his belly and then pull it away because he'll think that it's coming his way and take it out of your hands; you run that naked bootleg and then run it in.'

"Ten of the 11 guys in the huddle thought the play was going to Harmon," Gary said. "But Chuck did as Hayden told him because he trusted his coach. And he walked across the goal line with the winning score.

"Now, I've never asked Chuck, but if you go back and put some truth serum in him, he would probably tell you that he didn't doubt him at all because he's the guy who offered him a chance to play at the University of Iowa. He's the one who went to Chuck and said, 'Look, I want you to come to Iowa and be my quarterback.' So it's no surprise to me to see Chuck where he is today because of the belief Hayden had in him, the leadership skills he developed as quarterback and because of the tough, hard-working and humble person his parents raised."

Who do you believe in?

And are you someone who can be trusted?

Every day, you impact others by how you treat and interact with them.

Do you empower others?

Do you build others up?

Do you offer positive feedback and input?

Do you place trust in your children, co-workers, spouse, or significant others?

Do you coach rather than preach?

How do successful businesses grow? By believing in your team and nurturing them, says Atlantic Bottling Company CEO and Chairman, Kirk Tyler.

"The wrong kind of leadership is the person who says, 'I'm the boss and I know more than everyone else,'" warns Kirk Tyler (right), CEO and Chairman of Atlantic Bottling Company, pictured with his father Jim at the 1990 National Soft Drink Convention. "You'll miss out on a lot of good ideas when you think you're the only one who has them."

"And that starts with recognizing those who are on the front lines: your employees," he says.

On Oct. 1, 2016, the company's workforce almost quadrupled—from 220 to nearly 800—after acquiring new territories, including the Iowa cities of Ames, Mason City, Spirit Lake, Dubuque, Cedar Rapids, Quad Cities, and Ottumwa.

The growth impacted every facet of the company, including sales, marketing, production, maintenance, general office, warehouse, and truck loaders—to name a few.

"We pride ourselves on taking care of our employees—every employee—regardless of whether it's one or eight-hundred," says Kirk. "It starts with being fair to them.

"A phrase we use around here is 'STP' or, 'See the People.' Every day, I walk the plant not only to see the people but to let them see [me]. We heard from employees in territories that we acquired that I was the first management person they had seen in ten years."

Getting out and about, he encourages, is a critical asset to leadership. "I can get really comfortable in the office. I hate it, but I can get really comfortable," Kirk admits. "Sure, I can get on the computer and look at the numbers, but you really need to get out and talk to people."

In addition to being seen and heard, leaders encourage team members to speak their mind.

When preparing to serve the company's expanded territory, Kirk and members of the company's leadership team traveled the countryside to meet with new employees and gauge their satisfaction and assess their needs.

"Their first response was, 'Kirk, I'm doing great,'" he recalls. "'Then I'd ask, 'What do you need up here to be successful?' The reply would again be, 'Oh, we don't need anything.'

"At first I thought, 'Wow, this is great; we're doing all the right things!' Then I asked a few more questions. It's only then that I quickly came to understand that they'd been conditioned in the previous environment to not make any waves. And that meant not speaking their minds.

"Today, when I go in and ask how they are doing, they may still reply 'Fine,'" Kirk says. "But I push back and ask them to provide an honest assessment. I can't help if they don't tell me what they need. After all, I'm the person who can help. I don't care if someone disagrees with me. I'll take the time to listen and to explain, if need-be, what we are doing and the way we do it. But I can't help if I don't know what the need is."

That kind of free-flow of information is critical to success for any relationships, whether between spouses, teammates, or an 800-person staff.

"When you boil it all down, for us, success as a company begins with trust at all levels and between everyone," Kirk says. "If we're going to excel at what we do, every member of the team must trust each other. Only then will we open up and share what's truly needed to be effective and achieve goals.

"You have to trust each other; it's how you develop as a team and get better," Kirk adds. "We want every employee to act like it's their company. That they have a personal stake in everything that happens and every goal we achieve. We tell each other that people are going to make mistakes. But when they do, let others know right away. Don't hide anything. Don't cover it up. An injury, a damaged vehicle, or a driver who runs into something. Show people you care—that you want feedback, input—and that you're there to help.

"Regardless of the company, association or team, people respond when they know they are trusted, heard, and valued."

EVERYONE NEEDS A LIFT

Randy Edeker, chairman, president and CEO of Iowa-based Hy-Vee Inc., admires coaches who win. That includes Iowa Hawkeyes' head football coach Kirk Ferentz and his approach to work and life.

A few years ago, his wife Dawn challenged the supermarket CEO when she asked, "Who do you think tells someone like Kirk 'good job?'" When asked to elaborate, she repeated the question. "Who do you think tells Kirk Ferentz 'good job' or encourages him to hang in there when things don't go his way or the team's way?"

"After reflecting on that," Edeker recalls, "I began writing Kirk notes now and then telling him 'congratulations,' or 'Hey, hang in there.' He has to deal with the media and expectations and a lot of pressure. From time to time, that can be a challenge. And everyone, no matter where they are at in life or how high up in their career, can use an encouraging word from time to time. Be that encourager."

Believing in someone matters. Even when that "someone" is the leader of a Division I Football Bowl Subdivisioin member of the NCAA.

•

There's a leadership moment in his life that Jim Knuth will never forget. It was his junior year at West Marshall (Iowa) High School. He was the starting quarterback. Coach Doug Pinkham, never afraid to let his players fail, let the lanky athlete call his own plays.

It worked.

"As I reflect, this was the first significant leadership opportunity for me. In addition to being starting quarterback, I was delegated the responsibility of calling my own plays in the huddle, every down and even in the 'heat of the game.'"

"At the time, I certainly didn't think of it as a leadership moment," Jim admits. "I was just a high school kid competing in sports and trying to win games.

"But looking back, I do think this experience helped instill some kind of inner confidence in me to not be afraid to step up and put responsibility on my shoulders for the outcome of events or the team's performance.

"Looking back, it truly was my first true leadership experience. But once again, I was lucky enough to have someone who had confidence and believed in me."

•

Really good leaders know themselves pretty well, but it can sometimes be a lonely existence.

Leaders often believe in themselves when no one else does.

"Effective leaders are pretty honest with themselves," says University of Iowa president Bruce Harreld. "As a leader, you'll get blasted at times from the right and left. But you can manage that when you know who you are."

His wisdom comes from first-hand experience. Despite some academia experience (he taught at Northwestern University and Harvard Business School), Harreld's nomination faced criticism and controversy. Why? Because his "corporate" background (he held executive positions at Kraft Foods, Boston Market, and IBM) superseded his experience in academic administration. The Iowa Board of Regents, nonetheless, appointed Harreld as the University's 21st president.

"At times, people can be convinced that you're something you're not," he says. "Strong people can take criticism in stride because you know who you are."

One example Harreld gives of his confirmation battle were rumors that he was just solely about the school's bottom line and thus had little interest or time for the arts.

"I hadn't even started yet at the University when somebody wrote a letter to the editor of an Iowa newspaper. They said that clearly, if I was appointed president, the entire arts campus on the university was now in jeopardy and that I would probably lay a lot of people off and close it. And sell Jackson Pollack's mural.

"What's interesting about that is the same people who were saying such things didn't know that my wife has a very strong art background and my daughter has a Masters in Fine Arts and a son that works at the M.H. de Young Museum in San Francisco. I would be beheaded and quartered if I even thought that, and I wouldn't because I love the arts.

"So I go over to a guests home the same day the letter is published and say, 'How can anyone write something like that?' I'm then told by the person I'm speaking to—the former interim president of the University and former dean of the college of business; and he says, 'That's because I proposed it 15 years ago!' And I replied, 'What, how could you ever propose such a thing?' And he explained that here the university had this great piece of art and we didn't even know what we had and we hung it out in the elements for a number of years and then we hung it over the checkout area of our main library; turns out when we realized what we had and we didn't even know it and we had to pay for the insurance and then we have the flood; it's worth north of $100 million but it costs us a lot to insure it every year; just think of how many faculty we could pay if we monetized it.' I remember looking at Gary Fethke and saying, 'Your economics are impeccable but your values stink.' He laughed and looked at me and said, 'I know.'"

Rather than avoid rumors, turn to those who make them and address them head-on.

"I made it a point to meet people both during and after the selection process. Someone would say something in the press and I would say, 'Hey,

I just saw what you said. Can I come over and talk for a while?' Some of my best friends are people I met during that time. And always will be."

•

"Find a mentor or secure an internship with someone who is very successful so you can see how successful people operate and how they accomplish things. You can learn a lot from watching successful people. I looked to historical figures like Abraham Lincoln and Winston Churchill. Despite the adversity they endured, both accomplished great things. So my advice is to read and learn about others and about those who have accomplished great things."

TERRY BRANSTAD, U.S. AMBASSADOR TO CHINA

Derek Sivers, inspirational speaker and entrepreneur, says there would be no leaders if others didn't follow. The first follower believes in the person they emulate, thus making that person a leader.

Scott Raecker, executive director of The Robert D. and Billie Ray Center, believes that leadership can be over-glorified. After all, he says, there would be no leaders if there weren't followers.

"The first follower is an undervalued form of leadership," says Raecker. "It turns a lone nut into a leader."

A leader must embrace the first follower as an equal, so, in reality, both believe in each other.

"The first follower is the underestimated form of leadership," says Raecker. "Other followers follow followers and not necessarily the leader."

"Think about Hy-Vee," he adds. "Randy Edeker, the president and chief executive officer, doesn't teach every 16-year-old how to bag groceries, bring in carts, or interact with customers. They are being taught by some other 16-year-old. So, the question about a helpful smile in every aisle and workplace culture can't just come from Randy. I'm sure if he could personally touch all 85,000 employees that would be awesome and he would. But as more leaders follow, more people become engaged and are part of the movement and the culture."

It also becomes more difficult for the fringe people to sit by idly, Raecker adds. Those sitting on the sidelines must quickly decide if they want to be part of that movement or not.

"Sometimes it's OK for those not fully committed and who don't want to follow to search for another opportunity that better fits their goals and dreams," he says.

Following is an underestimated form of leadership, says Raecker. And he's quick to point out that he says that based on personal experience.

"My life in many regards from a leadership perspective has been to embrace the role of the first follower," says Raecker. "Governor Robert D. Ray had the vision behind CHARACTER COUNTS! I didn't have the vision. I'm just the loyal follower who's been blessed with being associated with the right people in the right place to try to help it become a reality— from one 5th grade classroom in 1997 to a statewide initiative that's been recognized nationally as one of the preeminent leadership and character development movements in the country.

"I don't look at my leadership capabilities any less because it wasn't my idea or vision. Rather, how blessed am I to have had the opportunity to be involved in this great vision of Governor Ray and to work with these great people who work hard and who want to make connections? There's a lot to be said for being a follower."

•

You've got to have friends and a great support network – people who believe in you," says Gary Dolphin.

"Eddie (Podolak) and Bobby (Hansen) were in my corner from day one. And they as much as told me that as did Brooksie (Bob Brooks), (Ron) Gonder and (Jim) Zabel."

In those early days of joining the Iowa Hawkeyes' broadcast crew, Gary and the gang were a team of five. It wasn't without its moments.

"That many on a broadcast crew had never been tried before…where you have three Hall of Famers handling the pre-game and the halftime and the post-game and then Eddie and I coming on to do the game and to help with postgame. But we had to make it work.

"As time went on and Eddie and I earned our stripes and became more comfortable and confident, we let Brooksie, Gonder, and Zabel have their space. And they were all great about supporting us, too. They had confidence in us.

"At the same time, we treated them fairly and with respect. We believed in them, too, and where they were at in their career. You understand the situation where others are in and their frustration and disappointment."

Belief is a powerful force, essential to developing leaders and being a leader.

Bob Myers, retired CEO of Casey's General Store, says he was immensely blessed to have been in a position where he could influence others in a positive way.

"People want to know that you can be someone they can count on; that they can believe it," he says.

"Leadership is a process of learning by trial and error. It's also about aligning yourself with good bosses and good mentors.

"They don't even have to be someone you report to," Myers adds. "It can be someone from the outside that you fall back and seek their advice and counsel. And frankly, all leaders, regardless of the level you're at, have the responsibility to mentor subordinates and to do it in a positive way.

"Be someone others look to and look up to."

•

Relationships are also important to Jonathan Hayes. As an accomplished college and professional football player and former assistant coach with the Cincinnati Bengals, Hayes was attracted to wear the Iowa Hawkeyes jersey because of the relationships he had with fellow players, as well as coaches and support staff.

"They were sincere and honest, just as all leaders are," says Jonathan. "I knew if I went there I wasn't just going to go to this big place never to be heard from again. They would nurture me and make sure that I grew as an athlete, student, and, most importantly, as a person. Iowa believed in me from the start."

Bob Myers, retired CEO of Casey's General Store, was a driving influence behind the company's success. "Be someone others look to and look up to," he encourages.

Jonathan credits Iowa assistant coach Barry Alvarez for recruiting him to Iowa City.

"From the very start, he developed a great relationship with my mother and father," Jonathan reminisces. "When he would come to Pittsburgh to visit me, he would first make a stop to visit my father, who was in law enforcement. And after he'd stop at my father's office downtown, he'd come to my high school and visit with my coach; then we'd do a home visit where he'd spend time with my mother, father, and brother.

"He knew relationships were important to me so he spent time getting to know me and my family. A lot of schools and universities I visited had unbelievable facilities. But I knew the relationships I felt that the players, coaches, and staff had with each other would help me be successful."

MENTORS MATTER

The first place to look for a mentor as a young person, says Iowa State University President Wendy Wintersteen, is your favorite teacher.

"Get to know one you respect in a deep way and see if there's an opportunity to work with them in some capacity," she says. "I always think about the educational system in this country; it's an extraordinarily successful system. It's one that students can take advantage of, especially from a mentorship standpoint.

"Also, and I speak from personal experience, think about the spiritual life that you can have as an individual. How do you find that spiritual life and what's your connection to a church, or to the minister of your church, or members of the congregation? I think that's really important and a point of contact and connection that can last someone their entire life. So, you see special connections that people can build in two very formal institutions that we have in this country: education and your spiritual life.

"As I talk to students, I also encourage them to study leadership through the great books—to actually study it themselves," Wintersteen adds. "The book I recommend is by James Autry and a nice connection to Iowa, titled *The Servant Leader*. This is a book that can help anybody do better.

"The quote I always remember from the book is, 'Leadership requires love.' If students and young people decide to do reading, that book is a good place to start. It would be invaluable to them."

•

"Chuck and I would often visit after each game. If it was a loss, I'd offer general encouragement. It was all about trying to get him to concentrate on the positives, that he had a lot to be thankful and grateful for and to be proud of. As a brother, I'd get him to think about those accomplishments, especially during the tough times. He always had a lot to be proud of, even the tough loss against UCLA in the 1986 Rose Bowl. Whenever he faced adversity, I'd work with Chuck to focus on the positives. It's easy for people like Chuck and stars in their games and careers who've accomplished so much to forget about all those accomplishments when they have a loss. Reminders of better days and better games and better performances are important."

DAVID LONG, BROTHER OF CHUCK LONG

•

Jim Knuth of Farm Credit Services of America recalls that within 30 days of moving to Omaha, Nebraska, to take on a new role with the company, the person who hired him resigned. Ironically, he did so the day before the Knuth's moving truck arrived in Omaha from central Iowa.

"I remember coming home from work to sleep on the floor and my wife Dawn asked, 'What are we going to do now?' All we could do is try to make the best of the situation," Jim says.

Soon, another manager was hired for his department, only to depart the company within five months.

Within six months, Jim had two bosses come and go.

"About that time, someone walked into my office and joked, 'Well Jim, looks like you're the last man standing!' I was soon named the interim leader, and I did that for approximately six months. By this time, the CEO of our company had resigned. They made an announcement that no one currently on the team was qualified for the permanent job I was doing, so they left the position open."

Eventually, says Jim, the company hired a new CEO. He was Jack Webster—one of the people Jim credits for teaching him leadership, not management, and believing in his abilities and future at Farm Credit.

"He brought in a leadership team and for the next few months, I continued to serve in the interim role," Jim recalls. "Finally, Farm Credit's executive vice president Neil Olsen calls me in to his office and asks, 'Jim, what's your plan?' We talked for a couple of hours about my vision and what we should and shouldn't do. When we finished, he said 'Jim, you have the job. Let's go.'"

Today, Jim leads a talented and dedicated Iowa team from his office in Perry, Iowa.

"As I look back on the path that led me here, I'd like to think that I have a lot of flowery things to say. But that's not really the story of my career or leadership.

"It was having people like Jack Webster and Neil Olsen believing in me, encouraging me, and providing opportunity. Because they didn't have to pick me."

•

True leadership can turn a school, a business, an organization, from mediocre to great, says Doug Reichardt, retired chairman of Holmes Murphy and past board chairman of the Iowa Sports Foundation.

"But if leadership is so powerful and can be so beneficial, then why do so many people fail at it?" he asks. "Because people are paranoid of those who are better than them. As they climb the ladder, they surround themselves with people who are inferior to them.

"It's easier to be condescending. Things that might have worked in junior high won't work as an adult. Sarcasm is the lowest form of humor but it's easy when you want to make light of someone or to knock someone down—it brings the whole organization down.

"Good leaders make sure there is no room for this—no tolerance for this."

•

When asked who believed in him, Mark Vlasic is ready with the answer.

"Mom and dad," says the 1987 NFL Draft pick and former Iowa Hawkeyes' starting quarterback. "It was always about my two brothers and me. Everything mom and dad did was about their boys."

Now a senior wealth advisor living in Leawood, Kansas, Vlasic recalls growing up in suburban Pittsburgh and the role sports played in his life. His dad coached baseball and basketball; Mark also played football. He excelled in all three.

"I would say my approach to leadership goes all the way back there," he says. "One of the biggest influences in my life as a mentor and role model was my high school basketball coach. He was a guy that came to our high school from another school probably 90 minutes away where he taught. We always practiced after dinner because he needed to travel the 90 miles to get to our practice. That kind of dedication that you put in your life to help others succeed, there just isn't a better feeling than that."

Vlasic enjoyed throwing touchdowns, but nothing bested the feeling that came from winning as a team.

"Coach Fry and Coach Snyder and the staff at Iowa helped me learn the game and what team looked like and felt like," Vlasic reminisces. "You look at some of those teams in the 1980s that Coach Fry had, at least the ones I was on, and the bowl games we competed in and you look closer at the numbers of us as individual players, and then compare those to our competition.

"Often, on paper, it was a mismatch. But never once did we question [whether] we were going to win. We were always ready to win the next game that was in front of us. That was because we approached the game as a team and success together. We removed individual personalities.

"It was about the team and believing in each other. There wasn't a question in my mind that you're back there with guys trying to take your head off that everyone else was doing their job. They were going to make the right block and you were going to make the right pass."

PROFOUNDLY UN-PROFOUND

Retired Bankers Trust CEO Suku Radia has always believed in helping others do more and be more. Mentoring is something Suku does, and he encourages other leaders to do the same.

"One of the most important things you can do is believe in someone," he says. "I stress the importance of these things, including work-life balance and volunteerism…just the basic fundamentals; nothing profound."

That includes stressing that, no matter what you do as a leader, the most important job you'll ever have is at home, not work.

"When I was traveling and making stops at every Bankers Trust location as part of my farewell tour prior to retiring, I told folks that the most important job they are doing is not at the bank. It is in their home."

Suku recalled an interview with Dave Elbert of *Business Record*, former *Des Moines Register* business writer and a longtime friend of Suku.

"I was at Meredith at the time and he wanted to do a profile of me. I reluctantly agreed. So my friend Dave is taking notes and asking a lot of questions. And when we finished he looked at me and asked if there was anything else.

"And I said, 'Yes. Dave, you're a really good writer. So why didn't you ask me the most important question?' And he replied, 'I missed a question?' And I said, 'Yes, it's, how would I like to be remembered?' He looked at me and asked the question."

It was the easiest question of the interview, Suku says.

"I told Dave that I wanted to be remembered as a good husband, as a good father, and a person who cared about this community.

"Dave paused and replied, 'Suku, there is something wrong with your answer.' And I said, 'What was that, Dave?' He replied, 'Why didn't you mention your career?' And I said, 'Very simple, Dave. Because if you take care of the first three, the career will take care of itself."

So when it comes time to being a mentor, Suku encourages leaders to help someone take the next step professionally by helping them first understand the importance of personal fulfillment and accountability.

'I SEE A BIG FUTURE FOR YOU'

Randy Edeker of Hy-Vee Inc. wanted to be a government history teacher. He was also going to be a football coach. Then life happened. For a boy who started out as a part-time employee at the Chariton (Iowa) Hy-Vee, Randy quickly excelled in the retail grocery business.

"When I began working at Hy-Vee, I intended to be there a year and then move on," he reminisces. "A lot of times you set out thinking you know what you want to do and what your goals are and your direction. And then you find yourself in something that you love and that's the perfect fit and life changes yet again."

That's what happened to Randy who today serves as chairman, CEO, and president of the popular and successful supermarket.

Randy Edeker (right) with fellow store employees, Kirksville, Missouri (1990s). "I recognized pretty young that Hy-Vee was a good place to be," recalls HyVee Chairman, CEO and President Randy Edeker. "In retrospect, it wasn't the store director that sold the future to me and what I wanted to become. And it wasn't the corporate office. It was the full-time people in the store; it was my peers. Leaders are mindful of how they influence their peers."

"I recognized pretty young that Hy-Vee was a good place to be. But in retrospect, it wasn't the store director that sold the future to me and what I wanted to become. And it's wasn't the corporate office. And I'm confident that it's not those people, even today.

"Instead, it's the full time people in the store," Randy adds. "It's your peers who say, 'Hey, this is a good place for you to have a career;' it's the 35-year employee who says, 'You ought to think about this buddy; you're good at this; you could make something of yourself; you can do this and you can do that; look at all the opportunities around the company to move up, you ought to think about this.' Those are the people who recruit you."

Having someone believe in you, your abilities, and your potential is critical for success, says Randy.

"I remember the store director when I started at Hy-Vee in Chariton. He was good and nice to me. But he's not the one who sat me down and said, 'Randy, I see a big future for you.' It was those folks around the store that I observed and listened to. When you recognize that you like something, that you like taking care of people; for example, I like helping people and solving their problems; then you also find that if you have a knack for something, you tend to like it even more.

"Of course, being young and married at the time I took that first job with Hy-Vee in Chariton didn't hurt as a motivator," Randy added with a smile. "Failure wasn't an option. Necessity keeps you focused."

Randy also knows that it takes the right mentor for the right moment. People develop, they don't just arrive, he says, and that was certainly true for him as he looked to ascend the ranks at Hy-Vee.

"There was a time when I was in high school and I was coming to work for a company that promoted 'A helpful smile in every aisle.' The problem was I couldn't look anybody in the eye and say hello to them. And so when you come into a company like this, having that hesitancy is no longer an option because your brand is built around being friendly, open, and smiling. So you need the right mentor at the right moment. I was fortunate because at that time, I needed a mentor that would help me deal with the basics of leadership and speaking and confidence and the ability to begin even thinking about leading. And I did.

"Today, I will see something in a person—the possibilities and the potential—but they won't see it themselves yet. *So the first thing you have to do as a mentor is help the person see the potential within themselves. Mentors have served me well throughout my career because they are people willing to invest time and care.* They're special people who make those around them better."

•

"Hire good people. Then help them understand how you operate, how you want things done. Then get out of the way and let them do it. At first, this is hard to do. But if you've done your job, put in the time, done your homework and placed good people in leadership positions, it will quickly become easier to do. And your company will be the better for it."

Kirk Tyler, CEO and Chairman, Atlantic Bottling Company

•

Everyone experiences moments of doubt. It's how you respond to the uncertainty that differentiates success from failure.

For Des Moines University President Angela Walker Franklin, seeking the counsel of others is paramount.

"What was helpful for me during a period of doubting was to find validation somewhere else," says Franklin. "That may seem to be a strange way to say it but give it some thought. If you're struggling and you're frustrated that you haven't figured it out for yourself and floundering, this tells me that you've already exhausted your own internal resources."

Look to connect with someone else, she advises. Perhaps it's a trusted friend or counselor or maybe a parent, teacher, or confidant.

"Find the strength within and have courage and be vulnerable. Step outside your comfort zone and let others in. Ask someone else to take a look and peek inside. Given them an opportunity to see if their way of assessing and interpreting might be very different from yours.

As a therapist, Franklin used to see this in counseling. She would observe people at wits end.

"Those who could ask for help? Those are the people who found a way," she says. "Be vulnerable. Let others see you for who you are. Let someone else help you figure it out."

•

It was December 1997 and Scott Raecker was encouraged by neighborhood friends and fellow Rotarians to run for the Iowa Legislature. His initial response was completely dismissive, Scott recalls. He had a young family and just started a new non-profit with Governor Ray. And serving in the statehouse wasn't on his radar.

But one evening on a drive home, his wife Martha turned to him and expressed surprise that, at conversations earlier in the evening, Scott had been dismissive of repeated encouragement to run.

"It's a humbling honor for friends and colleagues to come to you and suggest you should represent them," Martha says. "You just dismissed them. I'm stunned."

"I just don't see how we have time for me to seek public office," Scott countered. "We have so many opportunities with the foundation, and I'm committed to the work."

The conversation soon changed to other topics. But the idea made the agenda for Scott's next meeting with Governor Ray.

"Before I could even get through the door for our meeting, I heard him ask, 'Is that you Scott? I hear you're not running for the legislature and work is the reason why.'

Obviously, someone had tipped the Governor off that Scott was being courted for elected office.

"He then proceeded to tell me to consider it and before I dismiss it to visit with Martha about it. So I did, and opened up the subject with Martha. And I said, 'Remember about the opportunity to run for office; maybe we should talk about it?' And she just looked at me with this plain face—she's a saint—and asked with knowing indignation, 'So you talked to Governor Ray today?' And I said, 'Yes.' And she replied, 'So what did he tell you?' And I said, 'Well, he said I should probably think about it and talk to you about it.' 'Did anybody else tell you that?' she asked. 'You did.' 'So you're going to listen to Governor Ray, but not me? You don't live with the governor.'"

Scott ran for office. And was elected in 1998. And re-elected. When he decided not to run again in 2012, he had been privileged to serve in the Iowa legislature for fourteen years. Along the way, a deep and abiding friendship formed with neighbor, friend and mentor Brad Peyton.

"He was one of the most knowledgeable political strategists in the state. He believed in me—managed all my campaigns. We went to the same church—had children the same age. He became like a brother to me."

While in the legislature, Scott had the opportunity to travel internationally. That included Bangkok, Thailand during one of the country's most severe economic downturns. Scott's delegation made it a point to visit a Bangkok slum inhabited by 40,000 men, women, and children covering an area nearly the size of Drake University in Des Moines.

"It was complete squalor," Scott recalls yet to this day with the same clarity as if he was still standing in its midst. "People were defecating in the streets adjacent where they cooked food. We went to an orphanage within this place. There were forty children about the same age as mine at home. I had such a sense of shame there."

Scott returned to Iowa with the pictures, smells, sounds, and experiences top of mind. It was a compelling moment for him, and he vowed to never travel internationally and see such squalor again without first trying to do something about it.

"I was telling Brad about all of this, and he asked what I was going to do about it as he proceeded to share a similar story about ahow he was compelled to make a difference in China. He and his family had been motivated to provide scholarships to support children in an entire village to attend school."

Scott Raecker (left) with friend and mentor Brad Peyton in Zhongdian, China (Yunnan Province). "We connected like brothers. We were deeply rooted in our faith and from these shared experiences, believed enough in each other and the calling that we created a non-profit organization called the Shining City Foundation," says Scott. "Brad was always a doer and his can-do attitude was contagious."

"That was just like Brad," says Scott. "We connected like brothers. We were deeply rooted in our faith and from these shared experiences, believed enough in each other and the calling that we created a non-profit organization called the Shining City Foundation."

The foundation works to enhance living conditions and provide funding for education for people living in impoverished areas. The foundation, largely with the initial backing of Scott and Brad, built medical clinics in China and, more recently, Uganda. It has also helped construct schools and dental clinics and either built or refurbished churches on every continent.

"Brad and I had a special kindship. We shared so many shared experiences," Scott says. "In fact, we enjoyed coffee every Wednesday morning just to chat about life and experiences and the foundation. It was a special time."

From 1997 to 2013, the relationship flourished. Then, one week, Brad called Scott and invited him to coffee on a Saturday morning.

"I knew he had been having health issues. Well, it was that Saturday morning in June of 2013 when he told me he had been diagnosed with pancreatic cancer. On Sept. 19, 2013, he left this world."

Scott pauses. A tear comes to his eye but he doesn't wipe it.

"During those three months that we had together at the end, he urged me not to feel sorry for him as he took great joy in his life and God's plan and recalled the many people he had served and the satisfaction that accompanied living out God's plans.

"And it was on the morning before the last day of his life; and we're visiting and he shares some things that he wants to make sure happens with Shining City. And he pulled me close and said, 'You know Scott, next Wednesday is going to be tough for you. But I'm going to be on a mountain top having a nice chat with Jesus. And I know you well enough to know that you're going to be feeling this huge void because we're not going to be having coffee. But this is what I want you to think about. The void is not there because I'm gone. The real void would have been if God had not brought us together, never had coffee on Wednesdays, never been neighbors and done all these things together.'

Scott pauses. "I miss him today as much as I miss my father."

Then Scott sits a bit taller and leans forward with elbows on the table and hands outstretched, strengthened again by the memories of his good friend and mentor.

"I was recently asked to name the mentors in my life. Pretty clearly for me, my mother, father, brother and sister. They offered guidance and accountability. But from a professional standpoint of who I am today, professionally Governor Ray and Brad: two of the most influential mentors and friends you could imagine."

Scott readily admits that as he ages, he dwells more on the definition of mentorship.

"I've never considered Martha my mentor. She's my spouse. She's me. We're one and the same and we come together through this spectacular thing called marriage. I don't consider her a mentor.

"But as far as advice, counsel, confidentiality, accountability, no one is there like Martha. And as I grow older, my children are mentors, they teach you things at different stages all through life like patience and being a humanitarian and just being a better person and putting others ahead of your own needs and wants.

"We can all do better when believing in someone else and learning from them. I know I have."

Listening is hard work. *Really* hard work.

Too often, when people do listen, they do so to respond rather than understand.

Of all the skills there are to command as a leader, listening is often the most difficult. Yet it is mandatory if you're going to be in a position to do great things.

REFLECTIONS

Who believes in you?

_____

_____

_____

_____

How have they helped you?

_____

_____

_____

_____

Write them a note this week thanking them and letting them know how much their faith in you matters to you.

_____

_____

_____

_____

14 Listen. Really. Listen.

A quarterback in high school, college and the Marine Corps, Coach Hayden Fry learned the importance of listening. He taught his coaches to value it, too. To truly understand, he reasoned, one must gather all of the information. And for players to truly trust their coaches, they must have input and, above all else, believe it's heard and considered.

When it comes to being a leader and making a decision, the debate is very important. And that takes listening, says Suku Radia, who retired in December 2017 as Chief Executive Officer of the Des Moines-based Bankers Trust Company.

The skill for a great leader is simple, he says. It's listening. To make his point, Suku often tells the story of Henry Kissinger.

"He was a wonderful Secretary of State for Presidents Nixon and Ford," explains Suku. "He was on *Meet the Press* when Carter was elected, and he was asked, 'Dr. Kissinger, your family came to this country when you were two or three years old, your older brother and your parents felt that perhaps the persecution of Jews under Hitler was such that your father believed you needed to leave. And yet your brother doesn't have an accent but you still do.' And his response was, 'My brother spent more time listening than I did.'"

"I suffered from the same affliction," Suku adds. "My children will all three say 'Dad, you don't have an accent.' And then they will say, 'Dad, say this.' They give me a word to say and then they all start laughing.

"Of course I have an accent. That's because I don't spend enough time listening. For me, that's a real shortcoming. And now that I'm retired, my successor Don Coffin will do a much better job because he's a listener.

"Don't be like me," Suku adds with a smile. "Listen. Listening is a real skill and an important one. Master it and you'll go far."

•

Listening is paramount to leadership, agrees Iowa State University President Wendy Wintersteen.

When she first started in an administrative position early in her career, Wintersteen's job was to help solve problems people brought to the table.

"But I had a bad habit," she confesses. "I would listen and nod while they were talking. But I wasn't hearing what they said. As they were talking, I was busy solving the problem. That's because I was pretty sure I already had it figured out, even before they finished telling me about the situation or why they wanted to meet with me."

She learned that is not a very respectful way to work with others. It's not what people want.

"I learned that sometimes there's a very simple choice to be made or simple solution that can be arrived in short order," Wintersteen advises. "But frequently, the most respectful thing you can do is listen. Then, promise to think about what they have shared and that you'll get back in touch with them after you've truly had time to consider what you have heard. Because what they're telling you may not be at face value what you think it may be. Also, there could be some underlying message they're sending you in a very subtle way. And the only way you'll detect it is if you're listening deeply."

True leaders are helpers. Being of assistance begins with being an active listener and truly hearing what others have to say.

"If you can say that you'll consider what you've heard, then people feel more confident in the relationship they have with you," she says. "Then, regardless of wherever the conversation ends up or the decision that's made, everyone feels valued."

Wintersteen stresses the importance of listening. Failure to do so can have profoundly negative consequences.

"Listening is really the key. If you don't listen, then you really don't have a clear view about what is happening and you don't understand the next door that may be opening for your or the team you may be leading.

"Or, if you're not listening, you may not become aware of an impending danger or something that you should be aware of," she says. *"The key is to do less talking and hear as much as you can. You want to encourage people to come to you and share their ideas and their concerns. That won't happen if you don't respectfully listen to what they say."*

•

How tough was Earl Bruce, long-time football player and coach?

"He wasn't a tall man, but he commanded respect," recalls John Quinn, Waukee's Chief of Police and former Iowa State University quarterback who played two seasons in Ames under Coach Bruce.

"So we're in practice and Kevin Cunningham is on the team. You could set your clock that Kevin would get into a fight nearly every practice. Now Kevin was like 6-foot-7 and a mountain of a man with a heart of gold.

"One day in practice Earl goes up to him to call him out; he's poking his finger into the belly of Cunningham because that's about all the higher he could reach. And he proceeds to lay into him for not listening and not giving his best effort while continuing to ask Kevin if he wants to fight.

"Cunningham, who just towers over Bruce, stands there as Bruce continues to get directly in his face with profound resolve, all the while continuing to ask him to fight. Kevin and us as players are just standing there in disbelief.

"Then, Coach immediately swivels from a fighting posture to one of coaching and mentoring. He begins to talk passionately about life and about what it means to be a man and the responsibility that comes with it and treating people with respect, appreciating others for what they do and making sacrifices for others. He talked about all the coaches who bring their lunch box to the stadium and the weight room and film room each day so that Kevin and every player can be better. And that was the end of the fighting. It made an impression on Kevin and every player.

I'll always remember that day and what that episode taught me about leadership and doing things for all the right reasons."

•

Chuck doesn't hesitate when asked to tick off reason why he had an outstanding career.

"At the top of the list were the great teammates I had," he said during keynote remarks at the Iowa Summer Games Opening Ceremonies July 2016.

After that, five keys to success jump to mind, starting with listening.

Chuck Long and his father, Charlie, enjoying time together fishing on Lake Michigan.

- **Listen to your parents and coaches at all times.** My mentors in my life were my parents and my coaches. Listen to them. They will give you advice that you'll use the rest of your life.
- **Love your sport** – you have to have great passion to succeed. That needs to come from within – not from your parents or coach.
- **Work at it.** It should not take the threat of revoking Pokémon Go to get you out of the house. You should practice your sport and practice it all day long. It's getting out there on the playgrounds and playing with your buddies. Limit the screen time to 30 minutes a day and work on your sport.
- **Sportsmanship.** Pursue victory with honor. Learn it and live it. I

played with Barry Sanders, one of the greatest running backs of all time and classiest people I ever met. He never spiked the ball after a TD but handed it to the referees. He shook every hand of the opponent after the game and always said 'yes sir' and 'yes maam.'

- **Persist and preserve.** You're going to go through some tough times – maybe tomorrow, maybe next week. Be in the moment and you'll get through life and challenges with flying colors!

•

"What motivated me was the people who surrounded me. If I wouldn't have used the advice and listened to the people who were around me–my family, teachers, peers–I wouldn't have been able to make this last as long as I did. I was always willing to listen and to take into account the advice and knowledge and experience of others.

"Being a leader and traveling to the places you want to go starts with listening and learning from those who surround you. It really is that simple. Sometimes, you think you have to make a lot of decisions and that the burden is on you but in reality, the decision is made for you most of the time by just listening to sound advice. I was fortunate to have the opportunity to work with so many outstanding coaches and athletes.

"If you're a good communicator, you're probably going to be successful in most jobs and occupations. But if you want to truly be great, you have to be a good listener and focus on the basic, simple little things. This is what kept me in the position as long as I did."
JOHN STREIF, UNIVERSITY OF IOWA ASSISTANT ATHLETIC DIRECTOR (1972-2012)

•

"True leaders are always inquisitive," says Suku Radia. "They never stop asking questions and continuously seek advice and input. They ask for information and listen. They consider issues from all sides. *There is no such thing as a dumb question. The only dumb question is the one not asked.*"

LISTENING IS ADMIRABLE

"I admired Sandy Douglas for what he did while president of Coca-Cola North America—the way he handled constituents and people and the way he interacted with his direct reports and the Coca-Cola North America system," says Kirk Tyler, CEO and Chairman of Atlantic Bottling Company (Des Moines).

"I've seen very few people who are as good with customers—the Hy-Vees, Casey's, Wal-Marts—and even the politicians," says Kirk. "The soda and beverage industry is under attack all the time; first it's too much sugar; then we're bad for bones. Sandy doesn't shy away from the criticism. Instead, he contacted the twenty groups who were our biggest opponents and arranged a meeting with them. He sat and visited with them for one, two, or three hours, or longer if needed. He wanted to know why they were opposed to Coca-Cola and the products we offer. And he listened.

"Now Sandy probably didn't agree with everything they had to say. But he created an opportunity for them to share what was on their mind and, just as importantly, to share information about Coca-Cola that they were not aware of. It's this transparency that helps leaders grow and be more effective.

"Listening to your harshest critics and being transparent is also an ideal way to improve. It can motivate you to look at what you think you know in a different light, thus creating new opportunities in places you would have never looked."

•

"To be a good leader, you must listen," says Angie Peterson of the Children's Therapy Center of the Quad Cities. "And not just hearing the words, but truly listening to what they're saying."

Peterson, who has been actively involved in helping families with children in need for almost 30 years, has learned that misunderstandings can happen when you hear just the words rather than focusing on the message.

"When you listen for the message, you can avoid conflict and have better working relationships."

Burning bridges seems to have replaced baseball as the national past time. No one leaves quietly when things don't go their way. Instead, they take to the airwaves or social media to air grievances, whether real or perceived.

The philosophy seems to be that if the ship is going down, all parties are going with it and screw the life jackets.

Bad idea.

REFLECTIONS

Identify three ways you can be a better listener. Try them. Jot down the results.

_____

_____

_____

_____

_____

_____

Who is someone you respect for being a good listener. Ask them what makes them a good listener. How can you emulate their positive example?

_____

_____

_____

_____

_____

_____

15 Don't Burn Bridges. Ever.

Character comes easy when you're running downhill. When the playing field is level. When the pieces are falling into place. When you have your health. When things go your way.

But it shines brightest and makes the biggest impression when things get scratchy. We'll all face setbacks in life. Obstacles will appear. Plans will get altered. Someone will say an unkind word about you. Make a comment about the way you look or act—for not drinking to excess or lighting up.

Your motives will be questioned. Someone will put you down or step over you or give someone else the starting nod. They'll appoint or elect someone else or break up with you or move out or assume. It's not a question of bad or unfair things happening to you. It's a given that you'll run against the grain at some point.

But true leaders and people of character shine brightest when circumstances don't go their way.

How have you reacted to adversity or bad luck? When someone wrongs you or fails to repay a debt or favor, how do you react?

•

"I believe in not burning bridges," says Mark Vlasic, who played college and professional football before becoming a successful wealth manager. "You never know how and where the people you interact with today will be part of your life, your business, your world later on.

"You treat people with respect. It would take a lot to burn a bridge.

You give people respect as a human being and you do everything you can to earn that respect back. Where people get into a lot of problems or challenges is when they expect people to give them that respect up front. You have to earn it."

•

"Lion's head coach Wayne Fontes and I had a good relationship and I understood why he traded me to the Los Angeles Rams after the 1989 season," recalls Chuck Long, selected by Detroit in the 1986 NFL draft as the No. 12 overall pick.

"That's not to say it made things any easier. But it was obvious they were changing offensive schemes, moving from a pro-style set to the run-and-shoot. It was about moving the team in a new direction and that wasn't all bad. At least Wayne had a plan."

So when he was traded and packed his bags for a trip to the West Coast, Chuck held it together.

"I didn't burn bridges on my way to Los Angeles," he recalls. "But the same can't be said for a lot of other guys who get traded in the NFL. And that usually comes back to bite them."

Often, the temptation to leave town deploying a scorched Earth policy is too tempting to ignore. Many athletes and employees have done just that.

Perhaps you've been let go from a job you truly loved. Or maybe someone else got a promotion that you believed you deserved. Or a relationship that you thought would last forever goes south.

When disappointment stings, resist lashing out. Burning bridges is a fine way to end up on an island by yourself and with no life raft or matches.

Resist trying to get back at someone or throwing someone under the bus when things don't go your way, Chuck adds.

"Leaving Detroit the right way is a big reason why Wayne brought me back to Detroit a year later," he explains. "It was significant that I returned to the Lions after the 1990 season in Los Angeles because it gave me a chance to keep working in the league.

"It's a hard league to stick. A lot of guys make the mistake of burning bridges when they think they've gotten the short end of the stick. I had built up a good rapport with Wayne and kept my head up when I was traded. That made Wayne feel good about me and about bringing me back. They needed a quarterback to fill a spot and I had a good sense of where they wanted to go."

Chuck says the Lions head coach realized that the run-and-shoot offensive scheme was not a championship caliber offense so he was returning to a pro style set. Turns out that system suited Chuck and his style of play.

"I was also at that point in my career that I could get them out of trouble as a guy who could get them a win if need-be without taking a lot of reps in practice," Chuck recalls. "I stayed in the NFL three more years because I didn't burn bridges when things didn't go my way."

•

Few voices are more recognizable to fans of college football than Gary Dolphin. But the Cascade native didn't end up behind the microphone by accident. It took tenacity, treating others fairly and leaving every door open, even after walking through it.

Gary pursued a broadcast career after attending Loras College (Dubuque) and Brown Institute (Minneapolis), eventually landing the play-by-play gigs for the Northwestern Wildcats and Chicago Bears. They were jobs he enjoyed doing, in addition to helping coordinate game-day television coverage for both teams.

So it's 1996, and he's following the search for a new play-by-play guy for the Hawkeyes and enjoying the heck out of it—when, out of the blue, he receives a call from Mark Jennings, one of the members of the search committee—a guy he knew from back in the 1970s.

"Which is a reminder why you never burn bridges because you just never know when one of those old friends or acquaintances throughout your life or career may come calling, whether its Tom Bay who called to offer me the job at Northwestern College or Mark Jennings who called me out of the blue from Iowa one afternoon," Gary says.

Jennings says, "Hey, Dolph, we're just curious as to why you haven't applied for the Hawkeye play-by-play job?"

Understanding the politics of the University and what that job entailed, Gary said he was flattered to be considered but already had a good gig going at Northwestern. He was also enjoying his time with the Bears and wasn't going to jeopardize it by applying for a job that's just going to pay him lip service by stringing him along only to say "thanks for applying" and then hiring Bob Brooks or Ron Gonder or Jim Zabel.

"Everyone assumed that the search was perhaps just a false front because at that time, WHO Radio waved a pretty long tail and was pushing for Zabel, and I knew that. Zabel was 70 at the time, so he would have stayed for at least another 10 years."

But Jennings was serious.

They couldn't consider A over B or B over C because it simply wouldn't sit well with the listening audience or the boosters. So Iowa was going to go out and hire a brand new play-by-play guy. They had also decided that Eddie Podolak and Bobby Hansen were the color guys they wanted.

"We don't want to change the mix of analysts we have, but we will bring in a new play by play voice and think you ought to apply," Jennings said.

"Well, that was certainly the hint I needed," Gary recalls. "I overnighted a tape to the search committee in September. Then, I went to Iowa City for a couple of home games as they were sifting through applicants to make sure they hadn't missed anybody.

"It was a couple of months later I got a call; it was right around Thanksgiving of 1996, which was a surprise because I had already figured that they had listened to my tapes and weren't impressed and thought, 'Well, that's OK...I'll move on.'"

But then he got a call from Jennings asking him to come down for an interview. Gary did, and for nearly two-and-a-half hours he was questioned about who he grew up admiring in his younger days. He took their questions for a couple of hours before being told that that they would get back to Gary with a decision.

"Another three weeks go by and I thought, 'OK, now they really are moving on,'" says Gary. "Then, on a weekday night in mid-December a guy named Roger Gardner called me from Jefferson City (MO) who, at the time, was president of the sports division for Learfield.

"We're on the line with each other and he was kind of hemming and hawing around. Meanwhile, I'm motioning to my wife that he's just stalling as he works up the nerve to tell me I didn't get the job. Yet, in the back of my mind, I'm thinking that certainly he wouldn't be calling 60 or 70 or 80 or 90 guys telling them that they didn't get the job.

"And just then he says, 'Well, I really don't know any other way to put this to you so let me just say this: that I'd like to offer you the play-by-play position with the University of the Iowa Hawkeyes and be the new voice of the program.'

"Of course, here I am, a broadcaster, and I'm just speechless. I had to stand there and let it sink in for a minute or two. Then, I gave the thumbs up to my wife and took the job."

Gary pauses.

"We held a press conference a few days later; it was a Friday the 13th—Friday, Dec. 13, 1996. We started the following year, 1997, and here we are, going strong more than 20 years later."

That's the power of maintaining relationships and not burning bridges. Ever.

Goals are tricky things. Set them too high and they become wishes—too low and they're meaningless.

Goals can be as unique as the individual who sets them. Some need goals that are very prescriptive. Others don't, preferring targets that are more generic but every bit as important.

For Chuck Long, the goal was to be a little bit better tomorrow than today.

REFLECTIONS

Is there a relationship in your life that needs shoring up? Which one? How will you get started? When will you get started?

_____

_____

_____

_____

_____

Have you felt slighted or passed over? Has your work suffered because of it? Who do you need to share this with and how can you move on?

_____

_____

_____

_____

_____

16 Goals Bring Focus

Goals need not be fancy. Just make them. Chuck's goals were to play for a big-time college football program. To play in a Rose Bowl. To coach a Heisman Trophy winner. These goals brought focus of mind and effort.

The world is a busy place. Messages of all kinds compete for our attention. Paths to travel lead in all directions. Voices come from all directions. Choices abound. Some are positive, others negative. So how does one cut through the noise and options?

Are you on a winding path filled with a multitude of exits and on ramps? Do you have wants but haven't taken the time to determine how to achieve them? Perhaps it's time to slow down, block out the noise, set goals and get about achieving them by sharpening your focus and effort.

•

"I love to talk about Hy-Vee and I love the company. Dad did, too, when I went to work for Hy-Vee. He saw it as a stable endeavor. I remember him telling me, 'Everybody has to eat.' What I've learned as I've moved into the CEO ranks is, 'Yes, they do, but they don't have to eat from our store.' It's a very evolutionary time for us and we must continue to evolve and adapt and never be satisfied."

Randy Edeker, Chairman, CEO and President, Hy-Vee Inc.

•

For almost 70 years, one important goal of the Children's Therapy Center of the Quad Cities (CTCQC) was to have its own building.

Angie Peterson, president and chief executive officer, had been a long-time volunteer and staff person for the center that serves children involved in an accident or struggling to overcome a serious illness and require rehabilitation.

In 2016, Peterson joined other staff and volunteers in making that goal a reality by purchasing a building that would become the new home of the CTC.

"We've operated under different names since our founding in 1949 but had always worked out of leased or donated space for our clinic," says Peterson.

By 2005, the center and its staff and clients were bursting at the seams. This included providing services out of a building that was a 1950s-era physician's office.

"So, you can imagine very small exam rooms for therapy space with just two "gym" spaces—maybe twenty-by-twenty or twenty-by-thirty areas. There was little natural lighting and just one, narrow hallway."

The center had "always done a lot with a little," Peterson says, but it needed a building that reflected the quality of work performed by staff and volunteers. So, it was time to make the goal happen.

"We embarked on a capital campaign and purchased our new building in September 2016," says Peterson. "But make no mistake: it wasn't easy. It took tremendous commitment and resolve."

•

"I had a very flexible job – I could come in at 8 in the morning or 3 in the afternoon. But every day, I had two deadlines and no excuses. I had work due each day at 6 p.m. and 10 p.m. Every day. No excuses. Responsibility builds character and sharpens the focus."

JOHN CAMPBELL, SPORTS DIRECTOR (RETIRED), KCRG-TV, CEDAR RAPIDS (IOWA)

•

Goals are not always easy to attain. Those most rewarding are often the most difficult.

"We talk a lot about the building because it's enabled us to take our organization to a new level," says Peterson.

But the goal wasn't just to have a building to call its own. The real reason for staying focused on ending rent payments was to better serve families.

"The building is one thing, but really it's about the people we serve—the children and their families—and our tremendous staff and board of directors," Peterson says. "When we decided it was time to make changes for the future, the new building was a critical part of the plan. With a new building comes a lot of new opportunities."

And, as is often the case with leadership, it came with added responsibility.

"The greater Quad Cities community has supported us for years and is helping us achieve our capital campaign goal," says Peterson with a sense of pride and resolve. "With that community support comes greater responsibility to be even better stewards of our resources and to grow our organization. What gives me the greatest satisfaction is knowing that we're doing that each and every day."

Peterson is keenly aware that times are tough for many families in the Quad Cities, a metropolitan area that includes Davenport and Bettendorf, Iowa and Rock Island and Moline, Illinois.

The blue collar cities struggle with the rise and fall in the economic fortunes of manufacturing and agriculture. It's estimated nearly 50 percent of the babies born in Rock Island County, for example, are believed to be to families that receive public aid.

"People are really struggling, and when you have a baby that's born with a developmental disability or delay, there are a lot of additional financial obligations that come with that," says Peterson. "The same holds true for families who have a child involved in an accident or those struggling to overcome a serious illness and require rehabilitation. There are a lot of medical bills that come along with that and they can really pile up. When you're working to keep a roof over your head, food on the table and utility bills paid, these day-to-day expenses can become overwhelming when you also have medical bills to pay."

Every day, Peterson comes to work, takes inventory of the center's great staff and resolves to stay focused on the ultimate goal: to change the lives of the families and children it serves.

Five-year-old Angie Peterson playing dress up at Grandma's house.

"We know we are changing lives; that the work we do is making life better, not only for these children by helping them overcome their challenges as much as possible, but for their families," she says enthusiastically. "It takes the burden off the parents to know that regardless of the type of insurance they have or ability to pay, their child is going to receive the needed therapy. That's just the thing that we as humans should be doing. To ask the questions, 'How can we help?' and 'How can we help every day?'"

Those who have never had a child with a disability or delay can sympathize with people who do have this situation in their life. But until you've personally experienced it, "I don't know if you can have empathy," Peterson says.

"There's a difference between sympathy and empathy. I'm privileged every day to be part of this work and to see first-hand what this does for families, like the family I first met years ago in the green room while working my first Easter Seals fundraising telethon campaign in the Quad Cities back in 1993.

"That family was not given a great prognosis for their daughter's future. Of course, the medical professionals need to focus on the reality of the situation and they don't want to give parents false hope. Parents hear the 'probably won't,' 'don't expect,' 'highly unlikely'; those are the things the parents who get that diagnosis or who have taken ill with some very debilitating consequences of an illness...they hear.

"What we try to do is not focus on the limitation but on the possibilities," Peterson adds. "And that one little girl whose parents thought of the things she may not accomplish...well, she learned to walk with the use of a walker and a cane; she went to high school and competed on the swim team; she graduated from college and is employed in the Quad Cities. She's our newest board member.

"What a testament to our work."

No kidding.

As Peterson reflects on her career—the goals the center's staff and volunteers have set and achieved—she considers herself fortunate and privileged just to wake each morning and go to work serving others.

"I'm so very proud of the history of our organization and, more importantly, excited about the future and where we're going," she says. "I look forward to the future and the differences we can continue to make for some pretty amazing kids, some of whom have overcome more challenges in life at the age of 10 then some of us will our entire lives. I'm blessed to be involved in this and to be part of their journey every day. It's humbling to see what can be accomplished when you have so many dedicated people who are all focused on one goal."

•

"Leadership is about following through and holding people accountable. There is nothing wrong with having high expectations."

JIM KNUTH, SR. VICE PRESIDENT, FARM CREDIT SERVICES OF AMERICA

•

Shortly after coming on board as police chief with the City of Waukee, John Quinn began making changes.

"We had work to do," he says. "I truly believe in leadership and the development of it and setting people up for success. It's an obligation of each leader. I have each member of the law enforcement team develop their leadership philosophy. It will change and grow and mature but the core elements will remain unchanged."

John also displays every organizational chart, then flips them upside down.

"I tell my team that I work for each of them; that's what's represented when you invert the organizational chart. You can't sit back and idly watch what happens. You have to be fully vested in making change. Each person has a voice and can influence."

John's philosophy is that you don't have to tell anyone that you have talent.

"Let actions speak for you; let your confidence and character show," he says. "A lot of people are competent and can do the job; but leaders also possess tremendous character. Do you walk the walk instead of just talking the talk? I've been privileged to have people take a chance on me and to allow me to take on leadership roles."

It's been fun ride with the Waukee Police Department, Quinn says.

"I've presented challenges to the team and they've embraced them. They find the good in everyone. It's also the fact that change is difficult from a leadership philosophy. I questioned everything that was done in those first few days after landing the job after my time with the Iowa Division of Criminal Investigation.

"Our goal is to be the most successful law enforcement department in the state. You can see it, feel it, touch it," John adds. "[It's in] how we wear the uniform and the character of the people we hire. You can see it

John Quinn and wife Lesa. "A lot of people are competent," says John, "but leaders also possess tremendous character."

in the leadership development and how the leaders care about the people they work for. You see it in the coaching and mentoring and that it's a team concept. You can see it and feel it in their contact with a member of the community. Each officer determines whether the touch will be good or bad, keeping in mind that we see people at their worst each and every day.

"I had someone tell me that they would have never imagined that the face of Waukee would be the police department," John adds. "We relish that comment because it means we're making a difference in people's lives."

•

You wouldn't think that a seasoned executive like Bruce Harreld—with time spent teaching at Northwestern University and Harvard Business School and in strategic management roles with such U.S. business icons as Kraft Foods and IBM—would be phased by throwing his name in the hat for the University of Iowa presidency in 2015. Think again.

Shortly after Harreld's name was dropped publicly, criticism surfaced. Chief among them was a fear that his background in the corporate world wouldn't translate in academia. Some were concerned that a balanced budget would trump all other considerations, leading to program and staff layoffs.

"I got caught up in everyone having a narrative," says Bruce recalling the early criticism. "There were those who were clearly upset with the (Iowa Board of) Regents and the process.

"Part of what I had to do was turn around and look at it from their perspective and with the budgets being what they were and some having not received a pay increase for three years, and here comes in this business person. I'd be pretty on edge, too."

Despite the withering criticism, Harreld never once thought about pulling his name from consideration.

"I had a goal and I just figured, 'Hey, I've been in a lot of tough and intense situations, like when I joined IBM, which was, at the time, in a much worse situation fiscally and there were riots and at times physical violence.' So having gone through a bit of that, perhaps I was prepared for it. Maybe not totally prepared but ready to manage it."

The key, Harreld says, is having a goal and staying focused on getting to the finish line.

"If you know what you're trying to get done, if you believe in yourself, if you can paint a more compelling future for the organization and highlight how you can help others get there, then you press forward," he says.

"Without that conviction and focus on the end goal, I probably would have backed out in a heartbeat if I didn't have good answers to those questions or believe in [myself] and believe that what we couldn't get it done. I had to listen to the criticism and see it from their point of view. But I had to channel that. Turns out no one else is always wrong and I'm always right. We all have a little bit of dirt on us. As a leader, we always have to own a little bit of the perception.

"There were some long days. I'd go home at night asking myself, 'Oh my God, I can't believe this' and it was really bad, and I don't drink but wish I did at times because it was that bad. But I'd wake up each morning, get out of bed and say, 'Alright, here we go. Let's do it again.'

"And then you start building relationships with people; they get to know who you are; they start helping you and then you build trust, then a team. Then things start getting a little bit better, and then they go crazy again."

But with a goal in mind, the pathway can be straightened, resources saved and employees retained.

REFLECTIONS

What is one thing you want to accomplish in the next six months? What goal should you set and what specific actions will you take to get you there?

_____

_____

_____

_____

_____

_____

Who do you know that would benefit from setting a goal? How can you lend a hand to help them identify and accomplish it?

_____

_____

_____

_____

_____

_____

IN CLOSING

It's been said it's OK to look back, just don't stare.

Same is true for looking ahead. Sure, leaders are dreamers. They consider and anticipate. They think "what if" and "what next." As Wayne Gretzky, the National Hockey League's most revered star, once advised, "Great players skate to where the puck is going, not where it has been."

But the present matters, too. As do the accomplishments and life's precious moments that quickly fade if they aren't recognized.

Don't lose sight of the past and present while setting sail for distant shores. Where you've been shapes who you are and is key to where you're going.

Just like those featured in this book, make note of what and who has influenced you and your frame of reference. Revel in those moments and relish your accomplishments.

Easier said than done.

Too often, we're speeding to the next event, planning the next activity and pursuing the next challenge. In doing so, we fail to take inventory of what's happening now and the many blessings we have.

But hard work and positive results are worth taking stock of, reflecting on, and feeling satisfaction in.

What have you accomplished that is noteworthy? What relationships are you thankful for? What awards have you earned that you take pride in? Stay in those moments and appreciate them. Be present in your accomplishments; take pride in them. Only then should you go to work on the next one.

Take this advice from Jim Knuth, Sr. Vice President of Farm Credit Services of America, to heart:

"Never forget that faith, family and friends are the most important things in life. I'm glad and thankful and love the fact that I have work that's significant. I'm committed to it and it's a big part of my identity.

"When people have the opportunity to balance their lives, they become more committed to the task at hand and the organization they work for. It's really the ultimate win-win."

•

Through thick and thin, Hayden always tried to keep things positive, recalls Chuck Long.

Hayden would actually get angrier at his coaches than his players. He hired great coaches, let them do their thing and then held them accountable. He let them work. He was not a micro manager. As long as they were successful, he left them alone.

Hayden was all about keeping positive in front of the players through thick and thin. He would do a walk-around during practice at all positions. If there was something to straighten out, he would. Bill Snyder called plays during practice, Hayden during games. He would point out obvious mistakes and you would repeat it until you got it right.

The beauty of having Coach Snyder call the plays in practice is it allowed him to be working his own game script in his mind; and trust me, he logged every play. He had a lot of trust in Coach Snyder during practice so he could roam the field.

Hayden had a philosophy that he didn't want players to leave the field, practice or game, on a negative note, even in a loss. And that can be hard to do, especially after the tough losses where it can be difficult to find something positive to say. And that was the beauty of Hayden Fry as he always would.

The other real cool thing about Hayden was the celebration of every win. Each victory mattered – he'd start the hokey pokey and allow us to enjoy the win, even if we had been favored in the game. Hayden would remind us that winning was hard to do at any level of sports. That why he did it.

It's hard to win and when you do, you better enjoy it.

Note from the author:

When I sat and interviewed Scott Raecker, he referenced ten ideas he had put to paper to motivate and encourage leadership in action. He prepared them for the Des Moines Business Record's 90 Ideas in 90 Minutes. They were too good not to share as they apply to everyone at all stages of leading.

— Aaron Putze

10 IDEAS BY J. SCOTT RAECKER

Executive Director, The Robert D. and Billie Ray Center at Drake University

1. Remember who you are

No business or leader can be all things to all people. Stay true to yourself and keep your organization in alignment with mission, vision, and values.

2. CHARACTER COUNTS!

Our character counts in everything we do. Recently, the issues of civility, ethical leadership, and character (the mission focus of The Ray Center) have moved from "nice" to "necessary" in many people's minds. From schools to the corporate boardroom to the highest levels of government, our character does count.

The Six Pillars of Character are not just words on a wall. They are a way of life. The Six Pillars (and any core values) should be thought of with "I" and "action" orientation. Each day I reflect on these concepts: *what can I do to act in a capacity worthy of trust, treat people with respect, be responsible for my choices and the consequences that come from them, be fair and equitable in my decisions, demonstrate a caring heart, and be a good citizen?* I'm not "pillar perfect" by any means, however, I strive to have my actions and decisions in alignment with the core values I believe are important.

3. Culture shapes character

Our colleague at the Institute for Excellence & Ethics, Dr. Matt Davidson, has 20 years of research to support the concept that culture shapes character. Every person in the organization shapes culture. Every action and behavior can be enhanced by clear communication of expectations, intentional habits, proactive mindset and accountability of self and others to shape a positive culture that creates optimal performance and fulfillment of both person and place.

4. Integrity – Without it Nothing Works

Harvard Business School professor emeritus Michael Jensen states in the article *Integrity – Without it Nothing Works* that integrity is defined as what it takes for a person to be whole or complete, AND, that integrity is like the law of gravity: it just is. This is wholeness with self and with others.

Integrity also impacts systems, processes, and organizations through wholeness of design, implementation, and use. If integrity is one of your core value words, read the article and develop a common understanding of integrity in your organization. If integrity is not part of your core values, it should be.

5. Focus on how to bring mission, vision, and values to life

Mission, vision, and values need to be actionable and operational in what you do. The intentionality of enhancing culture through assessment, data-driven planning, and professional development for self and others is critical to the success of any organization.

6. Care about your people, and make sure they know it

Life and work are complex. At some level, every business is a "people" business. Listen and show appreciation to your employees and your customers. Whenever issues come up internally for our team, I always try to articulate and demonstrate a 'family first' mentality. As important as our work is, family is more important.

7. Manage your energy in addition to your time

In their Harvard Business Review article, Tony Schwartz and Catherine

McCarthy share that time is a finite resource and energy is different. Energy is defined in physics as the capacity to work. Our human energy comes from four core sources: body, emotions, mind, and spirit. Our capacity to work, and the capacity of our co-workers, can be expanded and renewed by establishing specific habits to enrich each of the core sources of our energy.

8.   Love (is not a soft skill)

The power of love can be a catalyst to any business. Love life. Love what you do. Love simple things. Love complex things. Love your family. Love friends. Love people—all people. The essence of life is love, and when we can demonstrate this in our work it has a dramatic impact on others as well as ourselves. For me, passion for a cause greater than self is the fuel for love.

9.   Little things mean the most and can hurt the most

Details are important. Pay attention to the little things and they tend to not become big things—both with interpersonal relationships and organizational outcomes. As it relates to outcomes, I have a mindset that "everything will be alright in the end, and if something is not yet alright, it is not yet the end."

10. Enjoy the Miracle of Now

Perspective is important. In our work, we continually strive for excellence and the next great goal. It is important to also reflect and appreciate where we are and what we have at any given moment. Enjoy the miracle of now.

MAKE THIS CHAPTER THE START OF YOUR NEXT CHAPTER

These stories weren't captured just to remain static, confined to just ink on paper, a book that's read and placed on a shelf.

They are stories to motivate and inspire; points of reference forged through personal experiences and strengthened by trial and error that can help others do more. Be more.

Where do you want to go? What do you want to achieve? Who do you want to help? What person would you like to meet? What promotion do you want to attain? What relationship do you want to strengthen? What habit do you want to quit? What habit do you want to start?

Take a moment to reflect and anticipate the choices and connections you can make that will position you in the sweet spot when opportunity comes knocking.

Start small, but think big. Dream out loud. Consider your options. Gain the insight and opinions of others you respect, trust, and admire.

Write it down.

It need not be eloquent or detailed. Just write it down.

Studies prove that writing something down increases the likelihood it will happen.

Make this chapter your next chapter by getting involved in the things that matter to you.

Learn a new skill. Try something for the first time. Start a new relationship. Volunteer. Step out of your comfort zone.

Take a chance. Take the advice of those featured on these pages to heart.

Because YOU are destined for greatness.

– Aaron Putze

"You can find yourself in this story. The memories and experiences described are shared by so many. The book is a gift of joy."

SCOTT RAECKER, EXECUTIVE DIRECTOR,
THE ROBERT D. AND BILLIE RAY CENTER, DRAKE UNIVERSITY

DESTINED FOR GREATNESS

The story of Chuck Long and Resurgence of
Iowa Hawkeyes' Football

Relive the memories of the record-setting quarterback and Heisman Trophy candidate whose travels took him from The Tot Lot in Wheaton, Illinois, to some of the biggest stages in college and professional athletics. Featuring Chuck Long, Hayden Fry, Kirk Ferentz, Hap Peterson, Mark Vlasic and Jonathan Hayes.

By Aaron Putze
Foreword by Marc Hansen

**Available in print and audio through Amazon,
iTunes, Audible and select retailers**